the astrological
ELEMENTS

About the Author

Sally Cragin is a longtime arts writer and an astrologer who has also written for *The Boston Globe*. Her column, "Moon Signs" (written as Symboline Dai), has appeared in *The Boston Phoenix* since 1998. She writes the monthly forecasts in the Llewellyn Astrological Calendar and has been contributing to Llewellyn's Almanac for many years.

To Write to the Author

If you wish to contact the author or would like more information about this book, please write to the author in care of Llewellyn Worldwide and we will forward your request. Both the author and publisher appreciate hearing from you and learning of your enjoyment of this book and how it has helped you. Llewellyn Worldwide cannot guarantee that every letter written to the author can be answered, but all will be forwarded. Please write to:

Sally Cragin
ᶜ/ₒ Llewellyn Worldwide
2143 Wooddale Drive, Dept. 978-0-7387-1871-2
Woodbury, MN 55125-2989, U.S.A.

Please enclose a self-addressed stamped envelope for reply,
or $1.00 to cover costs. If outside the U.S.A., enclose
an international postal reply coupon.

Many of Llewellyn's authors have websites with additional information and resources. For more information, please visit our website at

www.llewellyn.com

the astrological
ELEMENTS

How Fire, Earth, Air & Water Influence Your Life

SALLY CRAGIN

Llewellyn Publications
Woodbury, Minnesota

First Edition
First Printing, 2010

Cover design by Kevin R. Brown
Cover images: wing and fire © DigitalVision;
    water © Comstock;
    plant © BrandXPictures

Llewellyn is a registered trademark of Llewellyn Worldwide, Ltd.

Library of Congress Cataloging-in-Publication Data
Cragin, Sally, 1960–
  The astrological elements: how fire, earth, air & water influence
your life / Sally Cragin.—1st ed.
    p. cm.
  ISBN 978-0-7387-1871-2
  1. Astrology. 2. Four elements (Philosophy)—Miscellanea. I. Title.
  BF1711.C68 2010
  133.5—dc22
                                    2009046838

Llewellyn Publications
A Division of Llewellyn Worldwide, Ltd.
2143 Wooddale Drive, Dept. 978-0-7387-1871-2
Woodbury, MN 55125-2989, U.S.A.
www.llewellyn.com

Printed in the United States of America

This book is dedicated to you, the reader.

CONTENTS

ACKNOWLEDGEMENTS

Many thanks to many people, starting with my mother Janet and my late father Donald, who were always interested in the study of stars, as were my aunts Linda, Joyce, and Judy; my "Libra twin" brother Hal and my late grandmother Shakie Manooshian Mirijanian.

I am indebted to astrology editors through the years: Sharon Leah, Clif Garboden, Peter Kadzis, and folks at the *Boston Phoenix*. Writers who have inspired and educated include Frances Sakoian, Robert Hand, and Sybil Leek and Penny Thornton across the pond, whose *From Diana With Love*, a kaleidoscopic account of being Princess Diana's astrologer, is the book I've studied most as it's provided invaluable insights into interpreting aspects and dealing diplomatically with challenging clients.

Thanks to teachers at Harvard Extension School including Professor Greg Nagy and Professor Maura Henry. Special thanks to my author cousin Susan Cragin for reading this. Also, none of this would be possible without my clients through all the years: thank you for sharing your lives and planets with me!

Finally, thanks to my husband Chuck, who suggested the original idea and supported the production of the work, and a grateful embrace for our children: Christopher Tigran, whose first word was "moon," and Jet Beatrix, who came into this world dancing.

INTRODUCTION

I am grateful to all writers, philosophers, and practitioners of astrology dating back to antiquity. I have learned and continue to learn from a variety of sources. There is not one human culture that lacks an astrological line of inquiry in their lore—we are all guided by the Sun, Moon, and planets. What I have found fascinating are the simple similarities that emerge among cultures that have never intersected.

In my own life, a family friend named Ruth Shepard was the first person I knew who had an interest in astrology and birthdays. Ruth had a strong inclination toward palmistry and, being a classically nurturing Cancer, could make everyone feel special on their birthdays. It was in her house in Fitchburg, Massachusetts, that I first saw the Rosicrucian ephemeris and various books about Sun signs. The ephemeris is a collection of numbers, symbols, and data I found fascinating and mystifying. Years later in my early teens, my father, Donald H. Cragin, at the *National Star* newspaper in New York, had an opportunity to interview a female astrologer living outside Boston. I remember going with him to this lady's house and looking at the astrology books in her library. What she said remains a blur on the viewscreen of memory but I do remember thinking, "I wish I understood this."

Yet, I never read my daily horoscope. I always found the writing bland and not specific enough. It would have been much more interesting to talk to someone who actually *knew* about astrology! My aunts Linda and Joyce came of age in the psychedelic 1960s. I remember well-worn copies of Linda Goodman's *Sun Signs* in their houses and highly intense discussions regarding birthdays of individuals in their social circle. In my mom's family, the dominant element is earth—out of the six in my mother's generation, there's a Taurus, Capricorn, and Virgo, and just to balance things out a Leo (fire), Aquarius (air), and Scorpio (water). I can't remember a time when someone didn't ask, "When is his/her birthday?" if someone new was being discussed.

Sun sign astrology is fabulously entertaining and, once you know a little bit, it's easy to start exploring others' personalities. What propelled me to create a text that highlights the elements was thinking about similarities among the three signs in all four elements. Having "primary source research" in my backyard for the earth signs made it easy to note distinctions, similarities, and differences about female Taurus, Capricorn, and Virgo. In the family, the Taureans pride themselves on their stubbornness, often characterized as "consistency" and "reliability." The Capricorn theme is "independence" and "not needing any help." The Virgo way of doing business is "taking care of details" and "paying attention to health matters." What's even more interesting is the interaction between members of these earth signs, in that when each of them is around an earth element of another Sun sign, their own characteristics are acknowledged, justified, and then—amazingly—heightened.

Elizabethans would have instantly understood the premise of this book: that we are guided by "humors" in a more general way than our specific Sun signs. These humors are referenced throughout William Shakespeare's work, and his consistent references are revealing. In his era, people surmised that one's personality was a result of these four humors being in or out of balance. The humors gave off vapors that affected one's brain.

So a balanced temperament was one in which all four humors (sanguine, choleric, phlegmatic, and melancholic) were in harmony.

And what are you? If you're an Aries, Leo, or Sagittarius, you're a fire sign. Therefore, you're hot and dry. The Elizabethans called this "choleric," ruled by yellow bile, violent and vengeful. Someone with a preponderance of fire sign influences operative in a chart would be considered to be dominated by these sorts of moods. We all know fire sign folks who are shy and civilized, masters of Zennish detachment and infinite patience, but somewhere in their nature is a choleric side, and knowing its presence will help you in your relationships.

If you're an air sign (Gemini, Libra, or Aquarius), you're ruled by blood whose humors are hot and moist. This so-called "sanguine" temperament is generally good-natured, benevolent, and amorous. The downside? Too well adjusted and not likely to take action.

If you're a water sign, Cancer, Scorpio, or Pisces, you're ruled by phlegm (cough!). Yes, it sounds unsanitary, but this is about five hundred years before paper tissues! This humor is cold and moist. The Elizabethans thought a "phlegmatic" temperament came with recessive characteristics and shyness . . . even dullness. Of course, if you're one of those three signs, *you* know this is way off the mark.

Finally, the earth signs, Taurus, Virgo, and Capricorn, are ruled by black bile. That's just what you think it is, and it comes with a cold and dry humor. The resulting temperament was "melancholic." This tendency can include gluttony, excessive nostalgia, and a weakness for regret.

My hope for readers of this book is that they will see themselves, see the people they care about, and come to a greater understanding and insight about dealing with their own impulses, obsessions, interests, and interactions. There is no one-size-fits-all depiction of astrology, as we are all a unique collection of facets and aspects. However, once you start thinking about the astrological elements, rather than twelve different signs, you'll have an (what some might think as unfair) advantage operating on planet Earth.

HOW TO USE THIS BOOK

Step one. Be curious.

Step two. Think about what you're like, who you like, how you act, who you're drawn to, what amuses you, what leaves you cold.

Step three. Start reading at random.

How to Use This Book, Take Two

Step one. Be curious about someone else.

Step two. Crave insight into their motivation and try to figure them out.

Step three. Turn to the pages covering their birthday season and start reading.

How to Use This Book, Take Three

As much as King Lear makes a case for the vastness of his personality, "containing multitudes," *Homo sapiens* very often follows a specific (and yes, amusing and nearly infinite) spectrum of personality types.

Astrology, which I like to describe as the second oldest profession, developed in all likelihood because the people of prehistory noticed that the mood of everyone in the tribe shifted when the great big Moon was fully visible in the night sky. In the intervening millenia, we find virtually every culture developing its own version of star-gazing, planet-observing, and omen-interpreting.

The Astrological Elements acknowledges the standard-brand, cozy/comfy Western astrological traditions and adds some special ingredients, including the fascinating chemical interactions that emerge from likely (or interestingly challenging) combinations.

I've divided the text into the four main elements: fire, earth, air, and water. Within those four elements, you'll find three signs. I have divided each Sun sign into the two grand Freudian traditions of "love" and "work." In my experience as a practicing astrologer, it doesn't matter if you never have an Aries lover if fate keeps handing you the start-but-can't-finish-things Aries boss. Likewise, if you're constantly drawn to quirky and amusing Aquarian partners, you're probably craving to know the simple stuff like "Will they *ever* settle down? Do they have to get *so* bored so quickly all the time?"

Each of the first four chapters deals with an element and the three associated signs. It's here you'll find commentary on parents, children, lovers, friends, coworkers, and bosses, in addition to the occasional quiz or sidebar. I also include shopping tips (astrology should be practical and fun), and potential career choices for each sign. Throughout each chapter on the signs, you'll find paragraphs on your most- and least-promising annual weeks for taking action (or lying low, or lying convincingly). This section is applicable for every year.

one

THE FIRE ELEMENT

Introduction

Where would the world be without our fire signs? They get people to-gether, take charge, get the job done, move on to something else, and on and on. This element is literally the most volatile of the four elements of the zodiac, with a wide range of movement and charm.

Some folks find fire sign people perplexing and unpredictable. They can be, especially when telling you how cooperative they are, and how much enthusiasm they have, but the next moment, they've wandered off on to another playing field to see whether maybe *that* game has the challenge and excitement they need.

As clients, I've always found that fire signs can listen with real in-tensity. Whether they retain what they've heard or want to put it into action is another thing entirely. In romance, you'll find fire signs very hard to say no to, once they're determined. The trick is getting them to stand still long enough to hear you out.

A Brief Overview of the Fire Signs

Aries (March 21 or 22 to April 20 or 21)

Aries is a cardinal fire sign ruled by Mars. Represented by the ram, Aries love to start (but usually not finish) projects, make great leaders (as long as there are followers), and can be incredibly generous. Confidence and impulsiveness live side by side in rams, due to that Mars influence. Generally, none of these traits takes a toll on their appearance. In their youth, Aries can be maddened (and carded) as their appearance takes a while to catch up with their years—for years. Aries rules the head, and they can be literally "headstrong," yet also capable of processing and moving past annoyances with alacrity. Aries with style, power, and initiative include David Letterman, Maya Angelou, Ethel Kennedy, and Marlon Brando.

Folklorical significance: Aries is associated with the spring equinox, or "vernal ingress." The "spring ram" was traditionally sacrificed in some cultures at this time and the stars in the Aries constellation include the formation Cassiopeia. Aries herbs are influenced by Mars. These include "hot" flavors or spices like cayenne, peppermint, horseradish, red pepper, and the secret ingredient for absinthe: wormwood. Landscapes connected with Aries include, of course, places where sheep are kept, fireplaces, corners facing east (as Aries is the first sign, which "rises" in the east), and hilly or sandy places. Think of the ram bravely clip-clopping up narrow and unforgiving ridges.

Leo (July 23 or 24 to August 23 or 24)

Leo is a fixed fire sign ruled by the Sun. Represented by the lion, Leos are happy being the center of attention and don't feel fully alive without an admiring audience to applaud their activities. The ready smile (but not laugh) is theirs. Theirs is the sign of kings, or those who would be. Loyalty, dignity, and generosity come with this sign, but remember, pride goeth before a fall. Some Leos learn that arrogance costs them dearly (though Leo will never quite believe it if you tell them they've been prideful). Famous Leos who enjoy their command include Bill Clinton, Britain's Princesses Margaret and Anne, Barack Obama, and Napoleon Bonaparte. Leo is proud and rules the heart, and all it represents.

Folklorical significance: Leo comes in the middle of the summer, when, in the Northern Hemisphere, the heat of July and August represents the Sun at its most intense. The Nimean lion, which leapt from heaven and was one of Hercules' twelve labors, refers to this sign; and there are particular religious rituals involving feasts and sacrifices called "Leonitica." The stars in the constellation include Regulus and Algieba. Leo is ruled by the Sun, so the herbs and plants associated with our home star include heliotropic varieties such as almond, calendula, lemon, marigold, peppermint, and sunflower. Leo locations include structures designed for defense or fortification; buildings used for theaters or performing spaces; dance halls, places for children, and locations that have literal fires (furnaces, fireplaces, or cooking ovens).

Sagittarius (*November 23 or 24 to December 22 or 23*)

Sagittarius is a mutable fire sign ruled by Jupiter. Represented by the centaur (half-man, half-beast), Sadge people love justice and are keenly interested in philosophizing. Finding them at home is difficult: they're happiest on a long trip. Social and solitary, Sagittarius can combine the humor of Aries with the confidence of Leo and put their own half-man-half-beast spin on it. This sign rules the sciatic nerve, hips, and upper thigh, and they are happiest if they practice a sport that utilizes those muscles (walking, hiking, biking, horseback riding, waterskiing, snowskiing, motorcycle racing, etc.). Well-traveled Sadges include Frank Sinatra, William Buckley Jr., Winston Churchill, and Joe DiMaggio.

Folklorical significance: Sagittarius is the last sign before the winter solstice and the shortest day of the year. The stars associated with it include the minor constellation Lyra (the harp), the most ancient stringed instrument, also connected with the archer. Vega, that beautiful bright blue star in the northern sky, is in Lyra. Though it has some connection with biblical characters, this sign comes straight from our wonderful Greek mythology: the centaur, or centaurion. Jupiter is Sagittarius' ruler and its traditional herbs include aloe, aniseed, apricots, asparagus, beet, dock, sage (which flourishes on Crete, the mythical home of Zeus, a.k.a. Jupiter), savory, and thistle. Places connected with Sagittarius are those associated with horses, so stables, riding rings, or trails—especially locations for cavalry. High ground or places with a great altitude are also Sagittarian locations.

How to Speak Fire Sign

Fire sign people are direct. Blunt sentences ("That's stupid," "Don't order the cake—it's really fattening") are their stock in trade. With fire sign people, subtlety is off the table so the good news is that you (their friend/lover/employee/family member) basically know where you stand. There's no waffling with fire sign folks; they serve up their conversation straight from the griddle.

Delicacy doesn't really work with them. If you go to them for advice about a problem you are having with a person or institution, chances are you'll be told: fight it out and then move on. This kind of direct helpfulness will fill sensitive water signs (or passive-aggressive types) with dread. Best not to share with them, if that's the case. But fire sign folks like to analyze and will enjoy your insights into other folks' motivations or, more importantly, weaknesses.

Don't be surprised if that fire sign friend who was so fed up with the coworker, the boss, or the job is happily back at work the next day. One huge advantage these folks have is an ability to process experiences quickly. But don't be surprised if they leave a job without giving any indication they were unhappy—for similar reasons.

Fire Sign Parents and Children

Most fire sign parents will be happy if their children show proficiency in an area, or are capable of mustering up enthusiasm. Fire sign parents are reassured if their children are socialized (with the exception of Sagittarius parents, who can be all over the map in terms of consistency) but can sometimes head in the other direction. If they were in a particularly risk-taking mode in their younger years, their tendency could be to impose control or consistency with offspring where they felt they'd had none.

Fire sign parents with fire sign children instinctively understand one another and also figure out where they need to draw that line in the sand when needed (i.e., to let go of expectations or hopes of controlling the offspring). Fire sign parents should be aware that their own temper or tolerance can be stretched to the breaking point at an earlier interval—and nothing will make an earth or water sign child more hurt and confused than not having that early warning signal.

Fire sign children who do not have fire sign parents often take great joy and delight in boundary-testing. That fizzy temper that erupts without warning can be a fire sign attribute. So can impulse control issues. The "HD" part of ADHD (attention deficit hyperactivity disorder) is something I think of as a fire sign characteristic. Fire sign children love to bounce on the bed, climb the tree, make the tall tower, kick the ball, and write gooey valentines to Mommy. Lots of passionate friendships will come and go, so participation in a team or group can bring out the best in a fire sign child.

Aries Parents and Children

From total involvement to *laissez-faire*, the Aries parent is willing to listen to a variety of opinions on child-rearing, and then do what comes naturally. Aries parents can be great initiators of activities for their children, but sometimes make the error that their child is just as capable of improvising in social situations as they are. Aries also are willing to let others participate in taking care of their kids. They're a hands-on sign, but only up to a point. When they're at their best, they understand that a variety of influences is healthy for a child.

One instinct that Aries ought to guard against is the impulse to process adult emotions or episodes in front of a child. Because Aries and the other fire signs come with a certain measure of, shall we say, excitability, Aries can be in a "respond/react/move on" mode that some children will not be able to follow.

But Aries can be the consummate leader for a family (genuine or adopted). Merce Cunningham (April 16), modern dance avatar, created a family-style dynamic when his dance troupe was struggling. And Charlie Chaplin (April 16), once he was married to the much-younger Oona O'Neill, produced a number of children who all led interesting lives, from actor Geraldine Chaplin to circus impresario Victoria Chaplin.

"Fun" can be an attribute for an Aries parent and their zeal for finding challenging toys or activities for their children. Ethel Kennedy (April 11), the widow of Bobby Kennedy, was sort of an über-mom model for America in the 1960s and 1970s. She had eleven children, the last born after Bobby Kennedy was assassinated. Her brood's biographies follow a wide-ranging path from David Kennedy's tragic drug-fueled death to the commendable environmental activism of Robert F. Kennedy, Jr.

Aries children sometimes need special patience, handling, and approval because of their own instincts toward impulsiveness. Aries kids are explorers who also like to keep home base in sight. They'll be brave and defensive if they have a little friend who's not being treated fairly, and they also don't mind being in the mascot position with others. Because they often look younger than they are for years, it is easy to make the mistake that they are less mature, but Aries is often eager for new experiences and curious about experimentation. By providing a lot of structure and routine for Aries—while explaining *why* there is structure and routine—you can manage your little runaway ram.

When you have Aries children, be prepared for a certain measure of trend-consciousness. The natural state of Aries is to start something, move on to the next thing, start something, repeat, repeat, repeat. It can drive an earth or water sign parent (or one with heavy influence in the chart) ab-so-lute-ly bonkers to keep up with Aries kids' sudden passions, or need for the latest thing. Another characteristic of Aries is that once they have something, and they're bored, they have absolutely no problem giving it away.

Teaching an Aries child how to be responsible with money is an essential lesson, and the folks with heavy earth influence in their charts are both better equipped to do this (because of being responsible with money) and more easily frustrated. Julian Lennon (April 8), the "forgotten" son of Beatle John Lennon (October 9), has had an intermittently successful musical career but has long toiled in the shadow of his famous father and (more indulged) half-brother Sean. John Lennon, for all his imagination and brilliance, broke up with Julian's mother early in the white-hot fame of Beatlemania and wasn't able to provide the consistency and nurturing Julian needed.

Leo Parents and Children

The king is in his castle and all's right with the world. Leo parents are fiercely defensive of their little cubs and will brook no judgment of their kids. Enormous amounts of pride can come from Leo parents—sometimes to the detriment of their kids, who have a difficult time keeping up or feeling that their efforts are appreciated.

If you are a Leo parent, check your patience and your listening skills. Lions have lots of pride and children who are working hard at mastery will need much nurturing so that they can accomplish things at their own pace. I have known some Leo parents whose children have actually exceeded their own talent and accomplishments, but who have never and probably will never get the full approval of the Leo parent.

But Leo parents can also set an example of doing for others as well as high achievement. The fact that Leo can deal with adversity and then carry on (often without too much whining) is a hugely helpful example to set. At their best, Leo parents can be in touch with their own childhood experiences (and thus can relate to their own child's developmental stages) along with living as responsible adults.

Leo children love to be amused, love jokes and tricks, and can find humor everywhere. However, if they suspect you are laughing *at* them (because they are pretty darn amusing), their kittenish faces will crumple in a frown and the claws will come out. Leo children also can have a mighty yowl when crossed. It takes an extraordinary lion-baby (perhaps a middle child?) to find the humor in their own exploits as children. Despite the pride that goes with their sun sign, Leo children and teens aren't necessarily fashion plates and I've known plenty who lurch into the world with ripped and stained clothes. However, their *hair* is usually done to the nines.

Take the example of the Queen Mother (August 4), Princess Margaret (August 21), and Princess Anne (August 15). All are Leos, all have that regal bearing, yet each is perceived differently by subsequent generations. The Queen Mother was born an aristocrat (yet still a commoner by the lights of the Windsors), and worked extremely hard at the business of being an accidental monarch. She passed on her own values of hard work and smiling-through-adversity to her eldest, Elizabeth, while Margaret, the younger daughter, was allowed to be girlish and irresponsible.

Margaret inherited her mother's tendency toward tardiness (unthinkable in royal circles), and often affected a "hoity-toitier than thou" attitude toward those in her peer group. Isolated from reality yet without a specific purpose, Margaret was allowed much leeway by the entire family once her clandestine relationship with Group Captain Peter

Townsend was made public (and then publicly disapproved of by the Archbishop of Canterbury and Palace administration).

Later, she had a glamorous but tempestuous marriage to photographer Antony Armstrong-Jones (now Lord Snowdon). When they separated she spent as much time as she could in the tropics, in her house on the island of Necker. Drinking and smoking were her chief indulgences. Later pictures of the once-stunning princess, particularly after a series of strokes, are a cautionary tale.

As for Princess Anne, she never received the "honeymoon" her aunt did with the public, nor the lifelong love affair the public had with her grandmother, but she has been an independent spirit for all her life. Her work with Save the Children has been prodigious and she is regularly voted Britain's hardest-working royal. Unlike her more sensitive and emotionally complex older brother Charles, a Scorpio, she has shown little interest in her public image and, like her mother, keeps her public utterances to a bare minimum.

And we're still waiting to hear about the fourth Leo in the Windsor mix. Princess Beatrice (August 8) is the eldest daughter of Sarah Ferguson and Prince Andrew. As she's only recently left her teens, it remains to be seen what her personality will be like. But the few official portraits show that she, like every Leo woman, looks stunning in a tiara.

Sagittarius Parents and Children

Sagittarius parents like independent children. Their M.O. is to set an example as mavericks and then balk when their child defies the status quo. Subtlety is not their strong point, however. If they have a questioning air sign, a sensitive water sign, or a literal-minded earth sign child, they may find themselves responding to questions that they've never addressed themselves. But Sadge always figures everything can be fixed with a good night's sleep.

Yes, welcome to world of Sagittarian parenting, where inconsistency can be consistency, but everyone has athletic shoes that fit. Sagittarius parents can be terrifically generous with their kids in some regards. They might encourage the child to wander, but then not be so sure about paying for the Outward Bound class. Sagittarius parents with water or earth sign children need to pay special attention to the messages they're transmitting.

Does your child seem confused or not able to follow your divergent path? Perhaps it's time to listen to what's going on with them. I knew two people with Sagittarius birthdays whose eldest son was a Cancer. This child could have benefited from Sagittarius' social instincts and ability to mix in with all kinds of company, but these particular Sagittarius parents had had so much upheaval in their own youth that they clung to stability. As a result, they unwittingly isolated their children.

If you're a Sagittarius parent, you may feel conflicting impulses within your own parenting instincts. You value independence but not to the point where the child is going to wander too far. But look at the advantages you'll bring to your offspring: an appreciation of other cultures in the world and a taste for exotica that—chances are—their peers will not appreciate. Sagittarius parents have no problem being emotional and sentimental, and when they are able to share those thoughts with their children, it strengthens the ties.

Sagittarius children can be pretty wild and very funny. They are also highly accident-prone at various intervals (e.g. ages 3.5, 7, 14, 17, 21, 24, and so on.)

Fire Sign Friends and Lovers

Smart, smart move. Everyone needs a fire sign friend, and everyone should sample a fire sign lover. These folks will be very helpful when you need to clear your head, get some perspective, change the subject, or take a break. They also don't mind deflecting attention and, if you need distraction, you've come to the right place.

Fire sign folks operate at a higher RPM than others. They make decisions quickly and assume you'll be on board. They will also not spend a lot of time insisting on their point of view (well, most of them; Leo will have more invested in this characteristic). Fire signs will also not be particularly sensitive to your precious, fragile feelings, and will be surprised if you take offense at any of their actions. Since they generally don't carry a grudge for long (they've moved on to the next project), they're always surprised when others do.

If you're an earth or water sign, or imbued with a healthy helping of those elements, having a fire sign buddy can be maddening, but psychologically helpful. At the end of the day, when they're tapping their feet after listening to your specific list of grievances with a person or situation, they can sum it up with a shrug of their shoulders and the response, "What are you going to do? Hey, are you hungry?"

If you are a fire sign, you'll probably recognize aspects of yourself. If you are someone who lives with, works with, is related to, or is in love with a fire sign, this should help you at those times when you're thinking, "Get me an asbestos suit—stat!"

Aries Friends and Lovers

Everyone should have an Aries friend. Up for anything, willing to try the peculiar food at the restaurant, quick with an opinion, Aries at their best is fun, fun, fun. They especially love coaxing others out of their shell and show particular skill at making sure everyone feels comfortable. This can be because of their willingness to launch into a risque story, or to pull a prank. Aries' childlike enthusiasm can quickly defuse tension and can awaken feelings of nurturing in the most hard-boiled onlooker. "I got you a cool comic book!" is something any Aries might say at any age.

If you've got an Aries friend, prepare for a roller coaster ride of enthusiasms. Like all the fire signs, caring deeply about a cause, person, project, or preoccupation is a hallmark. Usually these passions are quick to erupt, quicker to boil, and quick to be replaced. Consistency is the biggest challenge for these liveliest members of the zodiac.

Because Aries is the first sign, they have a childlike affect, which they have no problem exploiting. Silent movie comedian Fatty Arbuckle (March 24) was as big a star as Chaplin in his era. He was also renowned for his bad-little-big-boy appetites and behavior. Yet he inspired fierce loyalty from his closest friends (See "Astro-elemental Opposites" in chapter 7 for more on this hefty king of comedy). Author Kingsley Amis (April 16) is another Aries who pioneered a bratty anti-hero with his 1954 literary smash *Lucky Jim*, yet who was a friend to all, and actually ended his days in the abode of his ex-wife *and* her current husband.

Aries lovers can be outrageous in their passions and will court a lover with some special item from childhood—an Easy-Bake Oven for a Cancer inamorata, or a pair of roller skates for a Sadge intended. But you may be accused of robbing the cradle, as Aries lovers can retain a youthful look for years and years. That unintentional youthfulness can also translate into latency. Aries can be perfectly happy with their childhood and young adult preoccupations and feel no need to settle down (e.g., Warren Beatty, March 30). If you're hoping your beloved ram will pop the question and a number of years have gone by, you may need to be more direct. Aries usually has no problem with "direct."

Aries lovers can have confidence (that doesn't seem to be earned), and an impetuousness that can keep earth sign loved ones on edge. They can also be quick-tempered and sensitive to slights. They do not need the mulling over or reflection period. React, move on, react, move on.

Leo Friends and Lovers

In the course of researching this book, I canvassed a wide range of clients, friends, and family members. Virtually everyone had something to say about Leo. Here's a Gemini woman on the sign: "My spouse always says I am stubborn. (He should know about stubbornness, he's a Leo.) But I get along well with him: he has a can-do attitude and I love his creativity. He is also very loyal and steady. Leos are the fire sign I like best."

Here's a Virgo male: "The Leos I know/have met are often shameless self-promoters and self-absorbed. It is too easy to be in a conversation with a Leo and hear all about them for hours on end. Then they jump up and say, 'Gotta go!'"

And here's a Scorpio woman: "Leos used to excite me in a sexually magnetic way, but they really just want to look in the mirror. They are much better as friends."

At their most enjoyable, Leo friends and lovers can be a perfect fit, and still be all-consuming, as befits a sign ruled by the Sun that governs the heart. The themes for Leo from its relationship to the fifth house are children, pleasures, and public relations. Just as Aries can be childlike, so can Leo, to the extent that they are delighted when they're the center of attention and the arbiter of the rules.

If you have a Leo friend, you absolutely can't tell him or her what to do, particularly if the engagement or activity is public or a touch shocking. Think of Zelda Fitzgerald (July 24) frolicking in those fountains. A Leo friend is a big-hearted benefactor, and they can put more energy into their relationship with a constituency than with individuals. Think of centenarian poet Stanley Kunitz (July 29). He only became famous in his fifties, but spent much of the rest of his life involved with the Fine Arts Work Center in Provincetown, which benefited other artists. Robert Redford (August 18) used his movie money to buy thousands of acres in Utah for conservation purposes as well as founding the Sundance film institute.

Leo's nurturing side is a huge part of their personality and they will be very, very vexed if you don't recognize that (along with, of course, their fabulousness). Take Alfred, Lord Tennyson (August 6): Britain's poet laureate in the Victorian age, but renowned as a family man who also encouraged and nurtured younger poets. *Noblesse oblige* is a Leo trait.

Leo lovers can, indeed, be happier looking in the mirror, but at their best they want you to be just as wonderful as they are, and enjoy partners who aren't completely "put together," shall we say. They can be passionate without being sensual, and sex can be an activity that's athletic and reassuring. And they *do* have that thing about Capricorns!

Sagittarius Friends and Lovers

Of the three fire signs, Sagittarius definitely is the most varied, the most flexible, and the least likely to need a lot of reassurance. If you're friends with a Sagittarius, chances are you met doing some activity or game or diversion. A chronically restless sign, Sagittarius is invariably the more eccentric member of any group. They like it if you share their passions, but it's not necessary for them.

You can learn a lot from a Sagittarius, as they often are skilled jacks and jills of all trades. Having a Sadge friend can provide a lens on the wider world and give you unusual insights. It's not a particularly sentimental sign, and not particularly noted for partnerships. Emotionally self-sufficient, Sagittarius is a maverick, happy to share their hobbies and preoccupations when asked, but unlikely to yack your ear off unless prompted.

A Sagittarius will make you rethink your ideas about the fiery element that rules Aries and Leo. With some notable exceptions (Frank Sinatra! December 12), Sagittarius is a sign perfectly capable of laughing at themselves and the world (Randy Newman, November 28; Woody Allen and Bette Midler, December 1). If you cheat at cards (or cheat in other ways), they will be very disappointed. Yet Sagittarius is also capable of "situational ethics," and they're the least likely fire sign to welcome emotional confrontation. Sagittarius doesn't need your approval and when they feel emotionally needy, they can be abashed. If you are friends with Sagittarius, plan on visiting out-of-the-way places. And if the journey is rough or complicated—that's half the fun for them.

If you're involved with a Sagittarius lover, keep a pair of crutches handy and an Ace bandage and do not fuss. Give them a long leash and be very independent when they need to go hang-gliding, or make another huge move. Also remember that Sadge has a high tolerance for eccentricity, egomania, and selfishness. I've seen many, many Sagittarius folks with lovers who behave childishly and selfishly—and the Sadge will come back for more. Being independent with a Sagittarian lover is a good thing, but remember that they're really tolerant, and occasionally oblivious. What bugs you may not penetrate their consciousness for years.

Most important: You can alter a Sagittarius' behavior by direct confrontation. You can inspire them by example, but Sagittarius is a sign with enormous endurance. What you see as problem behavior, they see as a lifestyle choice. Oh, and as regards that accident-prone tendency: their difficult months are late February and March, June, late August, and September. Those are times when you can say, "Slow down" with good cause.

Fire Sign Preoccupations, Obsessions, and Addictions

What is it about fire signs that they don't mind the occasional dust-up? Fire signs are drawn to situations rife with conflict, and will defend to the death their right to speak their mind. However, if you're working with a Sagittarius, you may have to tread lightly. It's a truism that what they need is freedom, and they'll get freedom on the job however they can. One Sagittarius man I know has been a passionate bicyclist all his life. He also had computer jobs that meant he had to turn up in a suit and tie every now and then. Dennis got into the habit of cycling the twenty miles to his job and changing into his suit once he was there. If he worked really late, sometimes he'd just crash where he was or get his wife to pick him up. While everyone around him was getting pastier and pudgier from the inevitable twelve-hour workdays and junk food regimen, Dennis got trimmer and fitter and faster.

Soon, his responsibilities increased, and before long, people all over the country were answering to him. At that point, he became a stay-at-home dad, which meant he was on-call around the clock. Not surprisingly, he gained weight. But in true fire sign fashion, he didn't mind a bit. He has the confidence that comes with the fire sign temperament, which basically says (no matter how delusional this is), "I can lose it when I want to."

Fire Sign Work and Careers: Choosing a Career That Will Fuel Your Soul

Fire sign folks can decide at a very early age that yes, they want to be a fire fighter or an EMT or a police officer—and then happily follow through. Those professions aside, there is nothing ignoble about fire sign folks having a variety of career interests and pursuits.

Fire sign people, and those with heavy fire sign influence in their chart, are most content in jobs where they can improvise, and where oversight is minimal (or where there is a structure and procedure in place that is so rigid there is no question of hierarchy). All fire signs can be excellent leaders or managers, but some may find the sameness of management tedious after a time.

Nevertheless, there are finely drawn differences between the fire element folks, and what makes them happy may surprise you. Where you should work, what you should do, and how you should do it are your questions.

Aries Careers, Coworkers, and Bosses

Tinker? Yes

Tailor, probably not

Soldier, definitely

Sailor, yes, if working in the boiler room (!)

Because Aries is the first sign, expect them to be the natural leaders of the zodiac. You can expect to find Aries in the captain's chair, or behind the chief's desk, or running the boardroom. Careers that emphasize bravery, leadership, decisiveness, and a charming, childlike ability to stick to one's guns are places where the ram will shine. I've known plenty of Aries (and Sagittarius) people who have chosen careers as firefighters or EMTs. Something about the mobility, constantly changing venues, and need for quick response inspires Aries.

Gracefulness is not usually a particular Aries trait, but occasionally Aries surprises everyone with their own reaction to accidents, clumsiness, and the unexpected event. Look at adorable skater Janet Lynn, who won hearts in Tokyo in the 1960 Olympics by laughing off her fall on the ice. Or David Letterman (cheeky grin, broad forehead) who has played up his gawkiness for decades.

Given that the sign rules the head, you might expect distinctive voices (also from Taurus, which rules the throat, and Gemini, which rules the lungs). Bessie Smith had a slow, sexy way of making even the most benign blues line sound highly suggestive. She also showed the Aries traits of leadership by being the leader of her own band—highly unusual for women at the turn of the last century.

Fellow performing Aries Marvin Gaye and Billie Holiday are also noted for being musical innovators and musicians who took full control of their "product" by overseeing production and arrangements. Unfortunately, that Aries headstrong characteristic also led them to a path of drug abuse and eventual death.

Aries *must* have a healthy amount of human contact to thrive as their own boss. "Healthy" can be defined as a workplace where the phones are always ringing and packages constantly being delivered, which would require a *generalissimo* to keep all the troops moving forward.

If you work with an Aries who's older than you, don't ever bring up that you think they're inconsistent or that they don't follow through. If they walk away, it's because a project is no longer worthy in their estimation, not because they've lost interest or aren't disciplined. If you work with an Aries younger than you, the smartest thing you can do is treat them like a very gifted and hardworking twelve-year-old. No joke—Aries have this thing where they seem just a little younger than anyone else. In fact, if you put an Aries in a room with a bunch of people younger but with different signs, the Aries will have everyone playing hockey with a crumpled soda can.

Encourage your Aries coworker on those new ideas they have (or that you have). If you need someone to shake things up on a project, Aries is your go-to person, but bear in mind that they are often quite happy conceptualizing the project and leaving it to others (like responsible earth signs or patient water signs) to follow through. Don't hesitate to adapt their idea for your own purposes. Chances are, they won't remember the details and have already moved on to something new.

Aries bosses can be fun and, at their best, their childlike enthusiasm inspires great loyalty in others (especially if they are also capable of follow-through). The best Aries bosses know how to delegate and gently nurture people to the next level. Because they're basically fearless, Aries is seldom anxious if they're the liaison between the workforce and the big bosses. Of course, they'll be happy to tell you just how brave they were in the big quarterly meeting!

If all else fails, Aries can talk. A significant number of entertainer/talk show hosts/broadcasters are born under the sign of the ram: Rosie O'Donnell (March 21), Sir David Frost (April 7), David Letterman (April 12), and Conan O'Brien (April 18). Since Aries rules the head, it's no surprise that these exuberant motormouths have risen to the top of the talk profession. This quartet also exemplifies another Aries trait:

a slightly childlike appearance that can include a domed forehead or the classic "baby face." Frankness and self-deprecation are characteristic of three out of the four (Letterman has mined his Lincoln-esque homeliness for years, while Conan O'Brien's favorite adjective to describe himself seems to be "freakish"). Drawing attention to oneself is one of the traits that make Aries so gosh-darn lovable.

In a related vein, some poets are perhaps as famous for their public readings of their own work as for their published work. This trio of literary Aries—Lawrence Ferlinghetti (March 24), Robert Frost (March 26), and Maya Angelou (April 4)—cannot be said to lack thoughtfulness or dignity. Their confidence reading their own work is world-class. Each writer found an audience by being direct as well as lyrical in their work. As Frost puts it, "The best way out is always through," which is about as emblematic an Aries comment as it gets.

Leo Careers, Coworkers, and Bosses

"There's no business like show business like no business I know" wrote Taurus Irving Berlin for fellow earth sign Ethel Merman (Capricorn) for *Annie Get Your Gun*. My money says that these two undoubtedly encountered numerous show folks born under the sign of the lion. Now, if you're a Leo and have no interest in performing (but like to go to movies, concerts, performances), you'll probably be saying, "Everyone thinks Leos are these big showboats, but that's not the case for me!"

Leo rules the fifth house of children, amusements, parties, kings, hearts, and live performances. There are lots and lots of Leo folks who do end up in show business, but the beauty of this sign is that they can turn the most recessive of career choices into an opportunity for performance. Leo enjoys a job where they can help others—the more the better—or proselytize a lifestyle. Advertising is a fine place for Leo, or the beauty industry, or hairdressing can be a satisfactory Leo profession. And they're even happier if they can own the shop and have a nice, neurotic, responsible Virgo to take care of the books.

Leo's jobs are ones that put them in the public eye, so teaching, sales, public service, or party planning will all provide satisfaction. So can acting or teaching—or just working in a theater or school. For every out-there, rooster-strutting Leo like Mick Jagger (July 26), Madonna (August 16), or Peggy Fleming (July 25), there's a quietly competent Leo who gets business done behind the scenes. Herman Melville (August 1), author of *Moby Dick*, wasn't much concerned with his reputation in his own lifetime, but had a driving need for adventure and independence.

Leo needs to feel that something is at stake, or that massive amounts of fun can be had.

Party planning is an excellent Leo occupation. So is working with children, either singly or in groups. As parents, they're fierce defenders of their cubs, yet also quick to keep their brood in line and on a short leash.

If you work with a Leo and you're an earth or water sign, don't *ever* think there's *quid pro quo*. Lions are graceful about taking your idea and expanding it into something usable. Some lions can do this so skillfully, they'll have you convinced that it was their idea in the first place. Leo can be a terrific supervisor, however, as long as they get credit for trifles. However, do not question their judgment. If they've got a case of the pickies, or are born close to the sign of Virgo (late August lions) and have a touch of the control freak, do not balk or get defensive. Leo is a sign that is more comfortable being right. You can get very far with them by saying, "That's absolutely true and—" and then start contradicting them. They won't notice. Honest.

The advantages of working with Leo is that they can make every day a party. Fun and excitement and unpredictability can be a boon to them in a way it couldn't be to a Capricorn or Scorpio. Leo bosses value loyalty more than the other two fire signs, and they can also show enormous longevity in a profession. (Aries and Sagittarius would find this tiring and need to stir up the routine regularly.) Leo bosses enjoy praise from their underlings, but not too much. They already have extremely positive self-esteem and definitely don't need it from you.

One major player in New England municipal politics is a Leo maverick: Mayor Lisa Wong of Fitchburg, Massachusetts. She was only twenty-seven, but had already run two agencies after earning a bachelor's and master's degree in economics from Boston University. This first-generation Chinese American daughter of a restaurant family got her first big job as the head of the Redevelopment Authority in Fitchburg, a former mill town faced with hard times. In just three years, she rehabbed an industrial site into a spacious in-town park, and transformed an empty forty-thousand-square-foot building into modern office and high-tech industrial space. Her next job was in Boston but during that period, she bought a turn-of-the-century Craftsman house in this picturesque city and developed deep and abiding friendships.

As 2007 dawned, and Fitchburg was chided by the state's Department of Revenue for mismanaging its money, Wong kept thinking, "Why isn't anyone running for mayor talking about fixing the city's finances?" Over a period of weeks, Wong consulted her family and friends. But her mind was already made up. She took out nomination papers that

Leo

Your challenge is to be productive and feel others are with you. Therefore, the times of year when you'll be at your most dynamic are your birthday month, plus late March and April, and Thanksgiving to Christmas. You will not be at your best in February, May, and November. However, those are transitional months for you, and if you've been needing a "reality check" on how you're doing, you'll be more receptive then.

spring and spent the summer talking to residents about a plan to turn the city's fortunes around economically. She swept through the primary, and that November beat a longtime city councilor more than twice her age. She won the general election with seventy-five percent of the vote and became the first Asian American female mayor in Massachusetts (and joined an elite group of under-thirty mayors nationwide).

What's the "Leo" part of this story? Leos can be natural-born uniters. Wong had friends in the Democratic party, but she picked up supporters everywhere she went, from a female-focused political forum in Seneca Falls, New York, to coffee klatches at the homes of retired teachers and other residents who were tired of seeing bad decisions made at the city government level. By going door to door, Wong built a dedicated base of voters who heard her message of economic reform and urban revitalization firsthand. Week by week, volunteers assembled at her Main Street headquarters, and donations of all amounts poured in.

"I didn't care if they changed the job title to janitor," she told one group of supporters while campaigning. "I just want to be the person who fixes things."

Sagittarius Careers, Coworkers, and Bosses

The Jupiter rulership of Sagittarius can bring an interest in generosity and benevolence, while the ninth house rules long journeys, higher education, and spiritual matters. Satisfactory jobs for Sadges would also involve some exercise that utilizes the upper thigh, in an ideal world. A wandering minstrel, perhaps? A jockey? The law profession attracts this sign (as it does Libra), and nonprofit organizations are enhanced by their Sagittarius employees who can remind everyone of the higher purpose of the organization.

Sagittarius can be a very informal sign, yet it is also the sign of bishops and the clergy. Scholarly pursuits Sagittarius (and those with strong Sadge leanings) enjoy would bring them in contact with world cultures and religions. A job that involves a touch of gambling and diplomacy would make Sadge happy, as would a job with real independence, where Sadge can work deep into the night and go skiing in the daytime. Of all the fire signs, Leo is the most likely to settle down early in terms of career selection, and Sagittarius can and should sample a variety of professions.

Sagittarius can work well on their own, but as it's a fire sign, social interactions with others should be part of their work routine. Sagittarius can take direction and be a good team player, but there's enough courage and independence built into the sign so that they can break out when they need to. Sagittarius has enormous tolerance for the quirky and unexpected and they love underdogs (Bob Barker, December 12, animal rights advocate and host of *The Price is Right*). They also don't mind being the exception or trailblazer in their workplace. A job where they're the only female or male in an otherwise male- or female-dominated profession wouldn't bug them at all. Because the sign is represented by the centaur (half-man, half-beast), Sagittarius is comfortable with shape shifting.

All Sadges should travel, and a job that takes them far from home can be a useful and inimitable growth experience. Genius record producer

John Hammond (December 15) had a lengthy career at Columbia and his musical discoveries ranged from Billie Holiday right through Bob Dylan. He had the unique ability to hear potential and genius in a way that the world would soon recognize—but he got there first.

If a Sagittarius is your coworker, expect imaginative solutions to problems and a very elastic sense of what a deadline is. Sadges think nothing of bailing on work completely if something more interesting gets their attention, or a mountain needs climbing, or there's a sale on water skis. Of course, they'll always ask you if you want to come, which is why it's hard to be angry at them for very long.

For the most part, Sagittarius is relentlessly (even awkwardly) honest and straightforward. They'd rather blurt it all out than hold back the part that may be called diplomatic. Witness Sagittarius Garry Shandling's late 1990s lawsuits with longtime manager Bernie Brillstein. Or fellow Sadge Woody Allen's break with longtime partner Jean Doumanian. Here's a real Sagittarian moment: Bette Midler's public disavowal of her TV show *Bette*, long before the network pulled the plug. As she told a reporter, "I got into a lot of hot water by saying I couldn't take it anymore." The actress admits, "But I'm not sorry I said it because it was the truth. I was singing, dancing, doing location shoots, and sometimes I didn't finish until two in the morning. I had no idea it was going to be that hard. It was like doing a little Broadway show every week."

Sagittarius coworkers are excellent in emergencies: they just get bored with some of the day-to-day. If you have an archer in the office, send them on the business trip. And bear in mind they may not be happy with the rules as stated. With a strong sense of justice animating many of their moves, they will have no problem bucking your authority if they think it's justified.

Sagittarius bosses can be fabulous and capable of providing a happy, healthy, humorous workplace. They may not be the tidiest of folks, and they may be a little scattered on the details, but that's what you're there for, right? Sagittarius bosses can always be persuaded that an office party will help morale—and the most Sadgey (if that's an adjective!) of them will see the logic of doing this during work time! Sagittarius bosses are pretty unpredictable, however, and if they're getting pressure from the people above them, they will try to protect the underlings from the capriciousness of the folks upstairs.

Seven Simple Rules for Sagittarius to Get Along in the Workplace

1. Know when your vacation is.

2. Gauge the tolerance for humor in the workplace before you start making jokes at others' expense.

3. Bear in mind that others will take this job more seriously than you do. Don't rub their noses in your ability to laugh things off.

4. When you get your next tattoo, be diplomatic about choosing the moment you decide to share it with others.

5. Given Sagittarius' accident-prone tendencies, keeping an Ace bandage in the bottom drawer is good preventative medicine.

6. Your definition of what's fair and their definition of what's fair could differ. If they think you're worth more than you think they are, no need to correct their opinion.

7. Pursue jobs calling for travel, even if it means you're just rolling around the states contiguous to your own. You'll appreciate the fresh air.

two

THE EARTH ELEMENT

Introduction

Earth signs are very likable. Not always lovable, because they're the element that most often digs in their heels, but certainly easy to get along with. They come in three flavors: Taurus, Virgo, and Capricorn. And believe it when I say there's as much disparity among them as similarities. They combine well with one another and can even have lasting love relationships, but often someone with another element will bring out their hidden qualities.

Earth signs are renowned for their will and endurance. Some would call it stubbornness, and every earth sign I've ever known will admit (after the fact) that they are stubborn. You do not want to wrangle with them without a cohesive strategy laid out ahead of time. And for all their fondness for routine, they can be surprisingly capricious when it comes to acting on whim.

It's also a sign you don't want to rush. Let them move at their own pace, and figure things out on their own. Once they learn something, they know it well, but you can add to feelings of insecurity by acting as if they need to be speed demons about their task completion.

A Brief Overview of the Earth Signs

Taurus (April 20 or 21 to May 20 or 21)

Taurus is a fixed earth sign, ruled by Venus, the goddess of love, attraction, friendship, and good taste. Practical and for the most part steady, Taureans draw from that Venus rulership in their fondness for comfort and aesthetic beauty. They are supposedly team players, who lead only if they absolutely have to, but my experience with this sign is that they are willing to take the lead at the drop of a hat. Represented by the bull, Taureans are slow to anger, but once riled make formidable foes. God help you if they've got a grudge against you for any reason—these bulls never forget. Steadfast and endearing bulls include William Shakespeare, Ella Fitzgerald, Eva Perón, and Rudolph Valentino.

Folklorical significance: You may recall from your Old Testament the Golden Calf the children of Israel created during their wandering period in the desert. This image actually draws from an ancient Assyrian religious ritual using *Baal*, or the Bull. Numerous cultures used the image of the bull (inspired by the constellation) as a signifier of the mid-spring. For example, the May Day festival, with its May Pole and garlands, is designed to commemorate the sun moving into Taurus.

Virgo (August 24 or 25 to September 23 or 24)

Virgo is a mutable earth sign ruled by Mercury. Represented by the virgin, many Virgos are classic compulsive perfectionists whose eye for detail may delight an actuary, but annoy the rest of us. Exacting and finicky, Virgo are usually the first to point out some small flaw that no one else can see. Their self-image is often radically unrealistic. The world sees someone who's steady and committed to doing good, while Virgo often interprets their own performance as not quite good enough. They're really lovable once you get past the whining, and the best of them have a great sense of humor about their own eccentricities. Stylish and perfectionistic Virgos include Queen Elizabeth I, Michael Jackson, Salma Hayek, Greta Garbo, and Arnold Palmer.

Folklorical significance: Virgo is the last sign before the fall equinox. It is traditionally represented by a virgin lying down, holding a wheat sheaf in one hand and a plant in another. Don't be misled by the image of domestic indolence. Virgo is a highly motivated sign with awesome powers of organization. Virgo's association with Demeter (Ceres in Roman mythology) and her contained rage at Hades when daughter Persephone was kidnapped bespeaks an intense and focused forcefulness that can give as well as take away.

Capricorn (*December 22 or 23 to January 19 or 20*)

Capricorn is a cardinal earth sign, ruled by Saturn and represented by the goat. Caps are dogged, responsible, occasionally blunt, reliable, long-lived, and prone to gloom, although admirably steady. They're old when they're young, and young when they're old. Solitude suits them more than they'd have you think. Consistent and reliable Capricorns include Paul Revere, Elvis Presley, Elizabeth Arden, Johannes Kepler, and Diane Keaton.

Folklorical significance: We represent Capricorn with the goat, but the earlier version depicted a mythical animal, with the front half of a goat and the tail of a fish. Many early cultures used the goat as a sacrificial animal, and the Philistines of the biblical era related their partially piscine god, Dagon, with Capricornus (the Babylonians also had a half-fish god, Oannes).

If you're planning a dinner party, here's a strategy: Taurus, ruler of the second house of banking, personal security, and finance, is sharp at figuring out how to squeeze in one more person at the table. Virgo, which rules the sixth house of health, work, and service, will remember everyone's particular food allergy and eccentricity and will make sure the low-fat version is available. Capricorn, which rules career, limits, and public life, should be sent to the market to bargain with the butcher and examine every piece of fruit.

How to Speak Earth Sign

Planning, deciding, and declaring are all classic earth sign modes of communication. "The way things are supposed to be" is a perennial earth sign theme. At their best, earth signs show commendable levels of organization, and are usually very quick to say, "Okay, what's the plan?"—and then start telling you what the plan is.

Earth signs notice details and small features and facets of others' behavior, or, more usually, dress and appearance. Earth signs are also quick to proffer opinions and assume you must agree with them because they have arrived at their conclusion using irrefutable logic and insight. Following through is an earth sign theme as well, and if you need a clean-up crew, look no further than your Taurus or Virgo folks. If you need a decorator, most earth signs are excellent at finding harmony in surroundings.

Earth signs often sound more decided than they are, and if you're the kind of person who is intimidated by people who speak in declarative sentences, you should bear this in mind—particularly when an earth sign person is bossing you around.

Arguing with earth sign people is often a futile exercise, unless you can marshal additional facts and corroboration. Even better is to cite irrefutable sources. One-upmanship is a perfectly fair strategy, and if your earth debate partner wants to talk about what this morning's local paper had to say about the economic situation, you'll win the round if you can quote from the *Wall Street Journal* or *The Economist*. Since earth signs are often highly conscious of hierarchy, you can go from adversary to respected source in an instant (more on this in the "Work and Careers" section of this chapter). Earth sign folks have an innate respect for authority, compared to fire or air sign people, who often view authority as someone to go around, or water sign people who view authority as essentially problematic and not attentive to everyone's needs.

Earth Sign Parents and Children

I have seen a few permissive earth sign parents and it always comes as a surprise. Earth signs put a great store into consistency, limit-setting, and other classically earthy pursuits. Earth sign parents can also be great celebrators of momentous occasions, such as holidays and birthdays. Gathering the clan at home base is always important for earth signs, who can take as much pleasure in cooking the family favorite recipe as they do with experimenting with other concoctions. An earth sign parent is always quick to ask if you'd like seconds, and also welcomes stray guests into the fold, particularly for Thanksgiving.

An earth sign parent is one who'll keep a scrapbook for the baby, including every single last receipt. An earth sign parent will also get that college fund started while the baby is still *in utero*. (Exception: some Virgo parents have a more *laissez-faire* attitude about money. While they may not start the fund, they will certainly fret about it!) As for Earth sign children: Let. Them. Grow. At. Their. Own. Pace. Especially Taurus and Capricorn. If a child of yours is born under an earth sign—and you are not an earth sign—you may be bemused and then frustrated at the child's strong will. "I can't do anything with them" is a comment I often hear from mothers of earth sign kids. "They do things at their own pace" is another comment. Patience is required for any enterprise involved with the raising of children, but having an earth sign child poses interesting challenges for parents who have inconsistent impulses.

Taurus Parents and Children

Okay, full disclosure here: my mom was a Taurus, and her mom was a Taurus (their birthdays were one day apart). Here's what I've noticed about Taurus female parents and style: the table must look pretty—candles, tablecloth, the good silver (as opposed to the everyday silver because, yes, Taurus women usually have collections of table settings), sparkling glasses, and then too many dishes to fit on that table!

Taurus female parents can be amazingly organized—at least in their heads. Taurus males on the other hand, can be the easygoing character in this mix. Andre R., an education professional, is a Taurus who works long hours as an administrator, and describes his own parenting style as "Easygoing." "But I get home at seven or eight o'clock at night and by that time I have no energy to manage anyone. This is why good parenting is a team effort." Spoken like a true Taurus, with the emphasis on working together. "My wife would say, 'Have you eaten?' but I'd say, 'Oh, look, it's six o'clock, are you hungry?' My wife would say, 'Did you get your homework done?' but I'd say, 'Do you need a ride over to a friend's house?'"

Nevertheless, there is one area where this bull takes the initiative, and that's cultural enrichment and travel. "I'm the one who says we need to go here, we need to go there, like Sturbridge Village over Columbus Day, or certain movies, plays, and concerts," he notes.

If you're a Taurus parent, you might err on the side of making sure things look good, rather than are good, but chances are, you'll have a big investment in making sure your kids are well rounded. If you've got a Taurus parent, it's important that *you* be consistent. Taurus parents are protective, and when they've been clients, my usual mantra to them is: understand your child is different from you and will not value everything that you do. If they want to spend money recklessly, or waste things, you can model good behavior, but nagging won't fly.

Protectiveness can definitely be a triple-edged sword, and I was amused to find that Baron Münchausen (May 11), the man who gave his name to

Münchausen syndrome, was a Taurus. This syndrome is one of the more interesting psychological disorders in that its sufferers induce illness in themselves or a child (Münchausen syndrome by proxy), in order to get increasingly intense medical attention. The original Baron told many creative and preposterous stories about his own adventures. He exaggerated with zeal and relish to the point where author Rudolf Erich Raspe published the tall tales. These included riding cannonballs and even traveling to the Moon!

Sturdy and consistent, the typical Taurus child is resolute, with a sweet side. They often have a soft spot for the underdog—a trait shared with Pisces. You may be surprised to discover your little Taurus' first friendships are with those who seem a little out of step with the other kids. Taurus is a highly loyal sign, though, and loves to be surrounded by a "team." Group activities are excellent for Taurus. It is absolutely not worth your time to argue with a Taurus child about trivia.

Taurus children can also have an eager-to-please side to their personalities, as well as unifying abilities. Adorableness is also another Taurus characteristic. I keep scouring the show biz heavens to find a better example of a Taurean winning personality than box office child star Shirley Temple (April 23). You don't have to have seen any of the movies to have a warm fuzzy feeling about this curly-topped moppet whose box office success also saved Warner Brothers studios in the dark days of the Depression. Taurus people have a knack for attracting money and, as your child grows up, if they want to go to art school instead of law school, or specialize in musical comedy instead of municipal finance—let them. Chances are, they'll find success in whatever they pursue.

Virgo Parents and Children

If you have a Virgo parent, you'll never be without tissues, cough syrup, aspirin and ibuprofin, vitamins, and cans of chicken soup in the pantry

(Virgo likes to cook, but loves convenience). Virgo parents are alert but their parenting techniques can range from highly permissive to restrictive and overbearing. Joseph P. Kennedy (September 6), the patriarch of the Kennedy clan, was, according to the numerous biographies of the family, ambitious and militaristic in his expectations of his children, particularly the males. One can argue that high expectations take their toll: Kennedy never fully acknowledged John F. Kennedy's physical frailties.

But a Virgo parent will also hang in there with children through difficult growing periods. If you know or have a Virgo parent, you may marvel at the certain level of obliviousness that characterizes the sign. They'll zoom right in on the details, and sometimes miss the overarching emotional story. "Sidney and I were going to the store, and then she said something mean to me" could prompt the response, "You were going to *the store*?! What store? The store where you have to cross the *busy street*? You *know* you shouldn't be doing that . . ." And on and on.

Precise and methodical, Virgo children can have quirky senses of humor and a real appreciation of the absurd. However, they can deal with stressful situations by channeling anxiety through their digestive system and can be noted for their delicate (or quirky) eating habits. But to show you the range of motion within Virgo, I can think of two Virgo men, both born on the same day. One spent years as a food editor, reviewing restaurants, testing recipes, trying exotic groceries and ingredients. The other is a highly placed academic, whose tastebuds atrophied at around age seven (this is conjecture, mind you), which means that his daily diet consists of cereal and milk, peanut butter sandwiches, and the occasional hamburger. Nothing green, nothing "weird" (like pasta), no fruits beyond apples and banana, and absolutely *no* vegetables. He's great company at a pancake house and has no plausible explanation for his eccentric diet, nor any particular reason to alter his habits. Consistency in eccentricity is a comfortable place for virgins.

Spending time with Virgo children can be a strain because they're very careful listeners. Virgo oldest children can fulfill the caretaker role naturally ("Did you remember to take your vitamin?"). Virgo middle children sometimes have conflicting impulses when it comes to caretaking. Because they're so aware of others' feelings, they sometimes expect others to treat them with the same consideration, which, as we all know, is seldom the case. My best advice to the parent of a Virgo middle child is to help them develop good relations with others without feelings of needing to please because they know what other people might like. Virgo youngest children often know what's best for others, and would never dream of telling them.

Capricorn Parents and Children

Material security is crucial for Capricorn, as is autonomy. Because people born under this sign are so independent, sometimes others can perceive their parenting technique as distracted or distanced. Capricorn (like Scorpio) has a skeptical side, and the wise child of a Capricorn will learn early on to provide information on a need-to-know basis.

Capricorns also like to understand the limits and parameters of their children. Chances are, they bought basic parenting and growth and development books the minute their pregnancy test came back positive, but Capricorn will be unlikely to consult these unless in an emergency. One of the attributes of well-adjusted Capricorns is their ability to plan ahead and do the practical work related to child-rearing. Because they're generally so self-sufficient, however, sometimes it's difficult for them to see that a child needs more—whether it's interaction, peer activity, or just plain downtime.

"Plays well with others" isn't what's usually said about these sturdy, tough-minded kids. "Could be a leader" or "Could excel if willing to try harder" is more likely. The truism I always find myself repeating when dealing with the parent of an independent Capricorn child (or a Capricorn Sun sign) is that they're "young when they're old, old when they're young." Because Capricorn is a cardinal sign, they have a built-in sense of direction. In another manner of speaking, what makes sense to them . . . makes sense to them. If they are heck-bent on a certain course of action, do not deflect. Capricorn is the long-distance runner, versus the sprinter—the solitary climber versus the relay participant.

Like other earth (and water) signs, Capricorn's favorite hobby can be summed up thusly: collecting stuff. But despite being a practical (down-to-) earth sign, sometimes others are mystified by what Capricorn views as a good investment. I've known Capricorns of both genders who collect everything from antique kitchen implements to comic books, to vintage clothing, to artifacts from other cultures (particularly those that relate to spiritual practices). And I have to conclude that two major strains animate this Saturn-influenced sign: a fascination with the era that immediately preceded the Cap's own childhood, and a persistent interest in what could be considered exotica.

Capricorn independence can manifest itself early on. You can't necessarily encourage a Capricorn to excel in any particular field, and if they do take an interest in something, your best strategy is to not gush. Capricorn are always very hard on themselves, and have exacting high standards. They're also skilled—once they decide they need help—at engaging assistance.

Capricorn Matt Timms, filmmaker/comedian in New York is also the regular host of a trivia night at a local bar that often includes a cooking competition (okay, a chili "takedown"). Now in his thirties, engaged in numerous collaborative ventures, Matt notes, "I wish I didn't have to do it all myself! I am getting a squad of fans together to work for me—my agent, a manager who loves me, and a slew of Facebook friends to spread the word. So far, so great," while adding drolly, "I'm the worst teammate on the planet—I've been fired from a large percentage of mediocre jobs. I think they really missed the point of Matt Timms."

Earth Sign Friends and Lovers

At their best, earth signs are steady and reliable. At their worst, flaky and not entirely honest. Gemini and Scorpio sometimes get a bad rap in the zodiac as being deceitful or prone to unnecessary drama, but believe me, in my line of work, I've heard rueful stories about all three of these would-be Steady Eddies and Edwinas.

An earth sign friend will be loyal, but is also prone to giving advice and feedback versus just listening. They will not understand if you get into financial difficulties, either through mismanagement of funds or an inability to live within your means. They will usually not push their friendship on to you, so if you want to have a relationship with these folks, chances are, you'll need to make the first move.

Earth sign lovers may need some guidance, but once they find out you like to receive tiger lilies on your birthday, and prefer ham to turkey for Christmas dinner, they will carry on for decades. Picking up on subtleties is not their strong point—nor should it be. If your earth sign buddy or beloved doesn't know what you need, you need to tell them. In simple, clear language.

Taurus Friends and Lovers

A Taurus friend is loyal and values your loyalty. A Taurus friend will think carefully about what *you* would like for a present, then finds the best possible version at the lowest possible price . . . and then feel guilty for bargain-hunting, hinting broadly that they didn't spend that much. As their friend, you can find this behavior lovable or predictable but you can't fault their thoughtfulness.

Be warned, however; Taurus requires a *lot* of care and feeding in one special regard: making plans. Taureans are set in their ways, so if you are to say casually to them, "See ya later," their brains are immediately buzzing with possible definitions of "later." Best to make specific plans or none at all. But Taurus can be excellent companions in a number of venues that include: antiquing, yard sale-ing, attending a free concert in the park, or any aesthetic performance experience. Taurus loves parties and will want to know what they can bring. "Whatever" is not an appropriate answer. "A twelve-pack of imported beer" or "chips" will usually net you a case of beer or the jumbo bag (or both). Taurus likes to have things spelled out and, if you cross them, their first reaction will be— well, red flag in front of the bull. Nostrils flaring, steam coming out of the ears, Taurus has a short fuse that can embarrass and confuse them.

If Taurus understands your shortcomings (i.e., you s-p-e-l-l them out), chances are they can incorporate their understanding into your worldview. Taurus likes to have a good time, and the classical (i.e., ancient) definition of their body type is actually similar to their totemic animal—short 'n' stocky! Skinny Tauruses are totally possible, but after age thirty, they can definitely get that earth-sign jowly look.

Taurus lovers appreciate how you look, want to like your friends, and want to feel part of the group. If you've connected with a Taurus, and you're a flaky or disorganized (but charming!) fire or air sign person (or someone with those personality attributes), you've hit the jackpot. Taurus is sometimes very, very hard to romance, despite their fondness for material goods and luxury foods; they may not immediately get the fact that you like them, but hang in there. For the most part, once they've evolved past a level of immaturity, they can be very loyal—no matter how much you abuse them. If one member of a lesbian or gay relationship is a Taurus, there can be a shared passion in home improvement and shopping to help shore up the empty spaces in verbal interaction.

Virgo Friends and Lovers

A Virgo friend would *never* criticize you . . . to your face, that is. These mercurial, bright folks are highly tolerant of others' shenanigans because the pain of losing someone in their circle is too much to bear.

Virgo knows when you are off your game and will ask thoughtful, insightful questions to see what's wrong. Virgo can also let their introspection interfere with being what's considered a good friend, which is to say, you may be the one keeping the contact going.

Victor, a Virgo client of mine for many years, has a generous helping of Virgo self-consciousness along with just enough detachment to analyze his own self-defined tendencies of "critical, analytical, measured, loyal. Continually desiring some sort of order or pattern. Prone to finickiness, sensitivity, critical nitpicking." Victor works in an academic milieu, where he interacts with a wide range of highly motivated individuals, and has very particular fondness for certain signs, including his own. Cancers and other Virgos are particularly attractive. Tauruses are next on the list. Cancers' interest in the home and desire for things *just so* in that space makes sense to them. Their desire for security also resonates, but they also seem to have a desire for new experiences that is appealing without being threatening. Aries and Scorpios are also attractive, but in a wishful kind of way, as in, "I wish I was [combative, passionate, etc.] like that." In the end, though, those signs seem reckless, even as they attract.

For Victor, some signs (predictably) are never his cup of tea. I've known Virgos who always have a Leo "best friend," but not in this case. "The Leos I know/have met are often shameless self-promoters and self-absorbed," he explains. "It is too easy to be in a conversation with a Leo and hear all about them for hours on end. Then they jump up and say 'Gotta go!' The Sags I know are just a bit too flighty. It's cute for a while and I get to take care of things for them. Then it just . . . keeps . . . on . . . going. Pretty tiring."

As for being lovers, these folks need to say what they feel *as* they feel it and stop the analyzing! A Virgo lover will have strong opinions about what you say or wear or where you go or who you spend time with, but getting to what they approve of can take a while. Bear in mind that the symbol for this sign is the virgin, and Virgo lovers can have a touch-me-not vibe. Big, sloppy passion is not their thing, and I've had plenty of clients complain about Virgo selfishness. My response is: What are your expectations and what makes you think they will comply without you spelling out your desires? Are you willing to walk if need be? This is a sign that comes with great and enduring beauty; folks with this birthday get cut a *lot* of slack! Lesbian and gay relationships with a Virgo on board are at risk for power imbalances. Virgo is a practical nurturer and doesn't always take emotional health into account. Virgo will always try to find a solution to every problem, and that can be taxing for the non-Virgo who just wants to vent.

One fascinating case study that dominated tabloid news for most of the 1990s was a pair of British performers, Virgo Hugh Grant and Gemini Elizabeth Hurley.

No, they're not together anymore, but for the time they were, both achieved stardom—and disgrace. Grant was a frequently employed quirky supporting player until *Four Weddings and a Funeral* catapulted his career into the white-hot glare of A-list celebrity. On his arm at the red carpet opening was his longtime girlfriend Elizabeth Hurley, clad in a one-of-a-kind Versace gown assembled with gilded safety pins. Hurley had just signed a contract with Estée Lauder, and though she'd spent the previous decade-plus toiling in B-movies, it looked like her American success would hinge upon a highly splashy, highly visible cosmetics campaign.

Smart, quotable, and attractive, the pair were feted and adored at various award shows and media appearances. Grant won a BAFTA award and a Golden Globe and immediately leapfrogged on to the A-list of bankable movie stars. But in the summer of 1995, when he was publicizing his first big American production, *Nine Months*, he made a fateful decision. Apparently at loose ends in Los Angeles, he picked up prostitute Divine Brown one evening on the Sunset Strip. Instead of going to a hotel room, the pair had an encounter in Grant's car and only attracted police attention because Grant kept hitting the brake pedal, turning the rear lights on and off. The resulting arrest was one of the biggest show-business scandals in recent memory, and effectively torpedoed the Grant/Hurley relationship.

Yet such is the resilience of those born under the ruling star of Mercury that both celebrities actually enhanced their careers after this scandal. Grant, whose public personna was fey, distracted, and thoughtful, actually improved his appeal to the young male film-going audience. A previously scheduled appearance on *The Tonight Show with Jay Leno* received Leno's third-highest rating to date. (Leno famously began the visit by demanding of Grant: "What the hell were you thinking?" Grant's response, a sheepish yet sly comment, "I'm not one to go around blowing my own trumpet," was catnip to the studio and worldwide audience.)

And though his subsequent film tanked—a boneheaded thriller called *Extreme Measures* produced by his and Hurley's film company—Grant continued to select projects that showcased his multi-dimensionality and thoughtfulness. As for Hurley, her feline, predatory charm was well exhibited in Mike Myers' *Austin Powers* series.

More recent tabloid reports have the pair continuing their friendship which now spans more than half their lives. Hurley, a true double-sided Gemini, has since married and had children yet continues to pursue television and spokesperson opportunities. Grant continues to make public pronouncements about the unsuitability of acting as a profession for grown-ups (Virgo perfectionism!). Hurley went on vacation in the Seychelles with her child, new husband, and Grant back in 2007 (note the unique Gemini ability to simultaneously maintain two relationships).

What do we learn from this pairing? Virgo's meticulous preparation and self-criticism will not be denied. Grant has earned a reputation as being a crusty interviewee, completely disinterested in the process of celebrity. The guileless, inarticulate, bumbling bachelor he has so often portrayed is at odds with his actual identity. Virgo has infinite resources for self-criticism and doesn't mind coming off as sharpish. As for Hurley, Gemini's ability to reinvent and improvise is a constant theme.

Capricorn Friends and Lovers

These folks make terrific friends. Their innate self-sufficiency can mean their emotional needs are minimal, and though they may not be the ones initiating outings or get-togethers, they know enough about themselves to welcome company so that they don't turn into complete troglodytes. Capricorn, like Virgo and Taurus, can also be a masterful planner when it comes to interesting outings. Though Virgo can be flexible on following a certain musician or band, I've known plenty of hardcore fans with May or January birthdays.

A Capricorn friend is an excellent companion on jaunts to the big antique show, or the museum, or any place where there is a lot of things to look at. A Capricorn is also good company on a trip that turns out to be more difficult than anticipated. Climbing mountains without map or compass, or hiking into thick woods can make Capricorn a little nervous, but they'll stick it out (albeit with a *lot* of complaining).

Capricorn has much endurance, although they may not notice the subtleties of romantic interaction (You: Was s/he flirting with me? Did you hear that? Capricorn friend: What? Sorry, I was listening to the band . . .). But they will be by your side no matter what you decide about a potential lover. As for *being* a lover, well, they tell me they're incredibly romantic but I am still waiting for one of them to give me their definition of romance! These are the folks who, as elementary school children, think a bop on the head is an affectionate gesture. And the fact that they are so darn independent doesn't always make them easy in a relationship. Since they often take a very long time to loosen up, having a preternatural maturity at an early age means they can marry late. If they have an early marriage that falls apart, they can go for decades without another relationship.

Capricorn will remember to pay the electric bill but may have to be reminded about special anniversary dates. The goats I know in same-sex relationships sometimes have taken a while to come to understand their gender proclivities. But they bring confidence and authority to a partnership, along with their deep-rooted independence.

If you browse in the back of this book and look at "Important Astrological Terms," you'll see an interesting astrological angle: the quincunx. For the most part, the rule about general astrology is that the sign next to you is a good fit, and the sign two signs away is a good fit. So Aries would have things in common with Pisces and Aquarius (the signs preceding) and Taurus and Gemini. Leo would share interests with Cancer and Gemini (preceding) and Virgo and Libra (following). Yet I see, time and time again, Capricorn making longterm, enduring connections with Leo. George Burns and Gracie Allen; Ari Onassis and Jackie Kennedy; Led Zeppelin's Jimmy Page and Robert Plant. Many, many Leo clients through the years.

How is it that two signs that seem to have very little in common find one another over and over again? The ideal Capricorn/Leo relationship is one where the Capricorn is the support system, the comforter, the cheerleader, and the biggest fan. The Leo needs, as we know, a certain amount of appreciation (Julia Child), which can run the gamut to adoration (Madonna). Leo can be impetuous, despite being a fixed sign (all about stability and determination). Capricorn can put on the brakes at the first sign of a skid.

On some primal level, Leo is fascinated by Capricorn's steadiness and finds this comforting. In this pairing, Leo can be the visionary while Capricorn figures out the nuts and bolts. Take the case of the Ari and Jackie pairing, a partnership that moved quickly towards marriage once brother-in-law Robert Kennedy was shot and killed in 1968. Leo in a crisis needs to know that the person they're leaning on is rock solid reliable. Or, as one wag commented at the time, "Jackie has a billion reasons for marrying Ari." Tabloid gossip had it that Onassis died before he was able to extricate himself from the marriage, thus providing an ample widow's estate for Jackie.

But if you want to see a most entertaining version of this duo, check out George Burns and Gracie Allen. Their show-biz personalities were that of patient, practical sidekick and flighty, addled will-o'-the-wisp. Burns kept his cigar smoking as part of the act so he could take a long, thoughtful draw while the audience convulsed at Gracie's wisecracks and preposterous commentary. Gracie, the Leo, always propelled the storyline along, both in their duologues and in their popular TV show.

I have also included Jimmy Page and Robert Plant. Can you guess who is the Leo? Hint: Leo is happiest when they're out in front and they have a passionate relationship with their hair. Jimmy Page as a guitar player based his technique on blues runs and riffs—traditional forms. But with his front man capable of singing in four octaves, these two Englishmen pushed one another artistically for decades, and represented the two great gods of Greek celebration: Apollo and Dionysus. Plant's flowing blond hair, confident strut, and sunny, sexualized affect exemplifies the Sun god's straight-up sexuality, while Page's darkly intense guitar style and riotous proclivities are pure Dionysian pleasure.

Earth Sign Preoccupations, Obsessions, and Addictions

Passion is an essential human characteristic, and how we manifest it ranges from the affection it represents to suffering. It's a thirteenth-century word, drawn from the Latin *passio* which means both suffering and the state of being acted upon. Earth signs can be tremendously passionate but may manifest their most exuberant side on behalf of precious things, animals, property, or inanimate objects. Ideas don't get them as riled up as tangible things—objects to reverence, touch, or even transform. Think of the folks you know and the ones who are in a perpetual whirl of home improvement. Is their Sun sign an earth element?

The cheap or off-brand version generally isn't of interest to these signs, although I can think of plenty of Taurus, Capricorn, and Virgo folks committed to shopping with a fistful of coupons. Do they bring their own bags to recycle? Not always—one by-product of the earth sign is acquisitiveness. We all live with clutter, and earthy people can acquire stuff at the same rate as other people. The difference is, they can't throw anything out, so the casual onlooker sees literally layers of material, all accumulating at a steady clip of sedimentation.

What do earth signs like? Taurus rules the throat, and usually will have a collection of necklaces or scarves or turtleneck jerseys. Virgo rules the lower intestines, and usually has a pharmacopia of digestive foodstuffs and vitamins or a health regime. Capricorn rules the skin and knees to ankles and can be extra indulgent when it comes to luxury care of the skin.

As for addictive or obsessive behavior—food can be an irresistible indulgence, and yes, the shortest way to the heart of (most) earth sign people is straight through the gullet. There's nothing as lovely as having a banquet buddy, and your earth sign companion will be an excellent choice. If that's your strongest shared interest, see if you can't put in a few walks around the block as well.

Work and Careers:
Choosing a Career That Will Fuel Your Soul

I have never—and I mean *never*, in decades of talking to people—had an earth sign client who had serious financial problems. Anxiety—definitely. But for the most part, earth signs are blessed in that their instincts towards solvency, or at least spending less than they take in, are very strong. Yes, they can fritter, but somehow the bills get paid.

So—what should you be doing with your life? We all need to follow our dreams and pursue the topics that interest us—that's a given. But what is a natural fit for you, and what can make you happy in the long run? Let's break this down into constituent parts and explicate the three earth signs in terms of their essential nature, character, needs, and surroundings.

Taurus Careers, Coworkers, and Bosses

Taurus is the second sign of the zodiac, ruling the second house of banking, personal security, and containers. Venus rules their sign, so professions having to do with Venusian interests (love, attraction, and friendship) are appealing to them. Taurus doesn't mind taking a long time to fulfill a training regime or getting prepared. Even though your symbol is the bull, which we most often think about as goaded by a bullfighter who's waving a red cape, the bull's natural setting is a large, open field—with a very sturdy fence. Therefore, Taurus can be content in a place where the boundaries are clear and indisputable.

Unfortunately, they can be turned topsy-turvy if those boundaries aren't there and there's unpredictability in the workplace. Some bulls pride themselves at never getting openly riled at the individual waving the red cape, but for the most part, Taurus prefers a harmonious workplace, one in which the hierarchy is clear and Taurus has a healthy dose of autonomy and authority.

I've seen Taurus people be very happy in banks, in financial institutions, working in the financial aid office of colleges and universities, working in antique stores or museums of antiquity, making or selling jewelry, and making or selling fine quality foodstuffs. As Taurus rules the throat, singing careers can be a natural for this sign, and several of my Taurus clients have mellifluous and pleasant voices (Taurus can also manifest stress in their throats and laryngitis is a common Taurus ailment). Being in charge is a comfortable place for Taurus—corralling a rowdy group can make them very happy. Other professions that would fulfill their need to make the world more beautiful include working with flowers or jewels, or in the hospitality industry or any job where speaking beautifully (singing?) is an essential component. Hatmaking and beauty work (which can include hairdressing) are also fulfilling.

Both Duke Ellington and editor Robert Gottlieb (both born April 29) have reputations for inspiring the people who work for them—in Ellington's case, the great jazz players of the 1930s through 1960s; in

Gottlieb's case, as an editor at Knopf and the interim editor of *The New Yorker* after the decades of William Shawn. Musicians and writers can be willful and childish, but easily inspired, and both men were sharp about bringing out the best in others.

But here's an easy career for talented Taurii: a profession in which they can use their voice. If you heard so much as five words from these folks, you'd know instantly who they are. Eve Arden, knowing best friend in countless movies, plus the wise and witty *Our Miss Brooks.* Leslie Gore, plaintive voice of teenagers everywhere with an astounding range and an ability to sell all kinds of songs, from "It's My Party" and "Judy's Turn to Cry" to "You Don't Own Me" and "The Look of Love." Need more? Barbra Streisand and Shirley MacLaine (who share a birthday). Katharine Hepburn, who made a patrician nasal honk witty and intriguing. If it's men you want, try Willie Nelson, compassionate cowboy with impeccable diction; Randy Travis, with his throaty baritone and rumbling resonances; and James Mason, whose breathy diction and eee-nunciation, not to mention the peculiar stresses he put on unlikely words ("Lolee-TAH"), are instantly recognizable, memorable, and still imitated decades after his death.

Virgo Careers, Coworkers, and Bosses

I've never met a Virgo who didn't regard themselves as an underachiever, yet who was by anyone's interpretation excelling in all different directions. Virgo rules the sixth house of health, work, and service; its ruling planet is Mercury, from which we get *mercurial*, and no surprises, finding a Virgo happy in a job is challenging. Virgo needs independence, approval (yes, you *do*), and enough autonomy. They will seek out opportunities within a company to do something faster or more efficiently, and then complain because they're overworked. Virgo can excel in a hospital setting or in an environment where there are new (non-social) skills to use. Because Virgo is at the end of the summer season (Libra begins at the fall equinox), gardens, field environments, or places where fruits of the harvest are kept make agreeable locations for them. Mercury's influence on Virgo means they're happy in jobs with a lot of back-and-forth such as interviewing, human resources, mathematics, accounting, even playing tennis! The message-carrying aspect of Virgo also predisposes some professions like speaker or lecturer, reporter, researcher, or data analyst.

Perfectionism is a Virgo trait, and if I were a company CEO, I'd definitely have Virgo people strategically located in my fiduciary department. You can count on a Virgo to take extra time on a task, and they will find the error that no one else would have seen. Where Virgo sometimes gets into trouble is when they get impatient with others who do not operate with those same high standards of getting things right. Ted Williams, genius hitter for the Red Sox, was widely disliked as much as respected: his standards were impossible to meet.

Genius Nebraskan billionaire Warren Buffet is born under the sign of the virgin and, according to biographers, one of his salient traits is a bottomless curiosity about the businesses he invests in. He bought Gillette Razor stock because he understood that razors men used as teenagers are the ones to which they are loyal for the rest of their lives. Virgo can sometimes seem to be a conundrum—to themselves. They understand and can even predict the behavior of others but aren't always made happy by having this knowledge.

My cousin Susan Cragin, a Gemini and a writer/lawyer, has observed this sign up close:

> I belong to a romance writers' group. Among those who write romance fiction, there are many Virgos. They have romantic leanings but are very work-oriented. Much of women's romance fiction these days revolves around practical matters. For instance, industrialists always seem to be falling in love with top-notch accountants. Financiers fall in love with inventors who have just invented the Next Big Thing. Virgos are great at writing this sort of fiction. Their only problem is that sometimes they are too fussy about the writing, and take forever to finish a book.

Virgo is a quirky sign who can usually charm people on the job—until they get bored, that is. I remember teaching an astrology class and hearing from an energetic Sagittarian lady who had the misfortune of being born into a Virgo family, all of whom seemed to exemplify the perfectionist, persnickety, picky-picky side of Virgo. In Virgo's defense, I will say that it is *much* too easy to bring out this side of them. If you're inaccurate in your conversation, inclined to generalities, they can be merciless as they correct you. What usually bugs most folks is that many Virgos forget to smile when they do this.

Some Virgos are notable for their charm and ease with others. Sean Connery (August 25) pioneered a variety of sexy, sophisticated, killer charm that hadn't been fully explored before his Scots burr-tinged James Bond. Ingrid Bergman (August 29) is another Virgo who could not help being charming and sympathetic in every part she played—

Virgo

As your birthday comes at harvest time, this is a transitional time of year for you, every year. Whether to leave a job, to change a job, to take on more responsibilities—these are all issues that could arise as you're blowing out the birthday candles. You'll be able to get good counsel and get a better perspective from Christmas through late January and late April through May. Times when you will not be seeing things clearly, or be overly touchy, will be March, June, and December. If there are personalities or changes in the rules or procedures that vex you during those periods, you could overreact. Wait until the next propitious period to take lasting action.

charm that hinged on an irrefutable dignity as well. Lily Tomlin (September 1) explored the Virgo *par excellence* aspect of her personality in the cackling character of Ernestine the telephone operator, but most of her characters definitely veered towards the quirky, eccentric, and self-conscious. These are aspects I've seen in every Virgo—and aspects that Virgos definitely see in themselves.

But the world doesn't always pick up on this. Bob Newhart (September 5) also explored the awkward, self-conscious, neurotic aspects of personality, first in his brilliant stand-up act and then in his successful TV series. If you need to contemplate some Virgos who are totally on the humanity-improving service track, look no further than Mother Teresa (August 27) and 1920s stockyard industry exposé writer, Upton Sinclair (September 20).

Capricorn Careers, Coworkers, and Bosses

As far as the zodiac is concerned, Capricorn *is* career! The third of the three earth signs takes the attributes of Taurus and Virgo and amplifies everything. Taurus admits they're stubborn—until they compare themselves to a Capricorn. Virgo admits they're super-critical—until they compare themselves to a Capricorn. This cardinal earth sign rules the tenth house of careers, lessons, and boundaries. Saturn is the ruler, and since Saturn is never about taking the easy way out, Capricorn never feels they deserve something until they've earned it.

Capricorn also rules foundations, so professions involving the practical side of architecture (building, working with cement or stone) can be satisfying. Of course, the original profession in which one worked with earth—agriculture—can also be a Capricorn pursuit, even in these modern times. Twenty-first-century farming is more reliant on machines than family members, so the solitude and patience that goes along with growing things can be a good fit with this sign.

Capricorn doesn't mind a small office, because their intensity level makes up for the paucity of surroundings. Capricorn can be successful anywhere—medicine, business, law—but where they really come into their own is in charge of their own business or company, or with full autonomy. Negotiating with a Capricorn can be frustrating—they have no interest in the social aspect of give and take. They generally know their price, their limits, or their abilities better than you do (maybe even your own), and there's no budging them.

Despite the need for freedom, Capricorns sometimes take a lifetime to get to a point of autonomy. I view my personal mission—depending on other things going on in their chart—with Capricorns as encouraging them to fly with their business idea and their entrepreneurial impulses. Because Capricorn can take a very long view, urging a Capricorn to go into business on their own is like trying to move a boulder with a pair of chopsticks.

Capricorn

You guys have the biggest adjustment to make as children when you realize the Christmas presents showered upon others can also stand in for your birthday presents. (Later in life, Capricorn actually appreciates the fact that they cut down on the fuss, but this is a bitter pill to swallow, and you parents of Capricorn children absolutely have to differentiate the birthday celebration from the seasonal festivities.) Good times for Capricorn to be at their best are their birthday month, late April through May, and late August and September. Times when you will not have the same perspective will be late March through mid-April, late June through mid-July, and late September through mid-October.

A Simple Guide for Capricorn to Plan Their Own Business

Okay, Capricorn, you've spent your time in the widget factory, or assisting a tyrannical, unpredictable boss. How do you know when it's time to fly?

a. You're working harder than any of your friends.

b. You're spending your time daydreaming about a business where you can make something durable, fix something, create something the world doesn't know it needs.

c. On the job, you find yourself saying this a lot: "No, the way you want to do *that* is to . . ."

d. You realize you've inadvertently amassed a decent nest egg, through sheer inertia.

e. Some Leo in your life says, "Have you ever thought about doing this?"

If you answer a minimum of two of these questions, I'd say you're ready to go into business for yourself. Step one is to figure out how much money you need to live comfortably, which includes lodging and health insurance. Step two is to decide whether you need to do this business in a space other than the space you live in. Capricorn is amazingly self-sufficient, and even if they work outside the home, they have a habit of bringing work home with them. If you're providing a service, or doing something on the computer, or even making something that requires a small workbench (versus a ten-thousand-square-foot factory), you probably have a corner. Step three is to make a sign that says, "I need to make X dollars per (month/year—you decide) by Y year (Y year being four years from the date of starting your business,)."

Step four: You're there! Step four-and-a-half would be to find that Leo (or encouraging air/fire sign person) and get a pep talk periodically.

three

THE AIR ELEMENT

Introduction

Bewitched, bothered, and bewildered are the people who deal with air signs and are unequipped for the rapid about-face, that's-not-what-I-meant tendencies of this charming and unpredictable population. Consider the wind—changeable and various—it's what we create when we speak and an essential aid to navigation. Æolus, the keeper of the winds, gave Odysseus a bag of helpful breezes to assist his voyage home. The idea of containing wind is eccentric, poetic, and ultimately absurd. Your typical Gemini, Libra, and Aquarian hearing this anecdote will snort (good-naturedly): "You wish."

Air signs are highly distinctive from each other despite having traits that the casual onlooker could characterize with a broad brush. Among themselves, air signs are highly sensitive to one another's individual traits. Thus, a Gemini can find a Libra inconsistent in impulse while a Libra and Aquarius can definitely see the two faces of Gemini. Neither Gemini nor Libra can contain, control, or guide an Aquarian—until the water carrier is good and ready.

A Brief Overview of the Air Signs

Gemini (*May 21 or 22 to June 21 or 22*)

Gemini is a mutable air sign ruled by Mercury. Represented by the twins (or Janus, the two-faced Roman figure), appealing Geminis with at least two well-defined personalities are Elizabeth Hurley (forgiving girlfriend/dedicated movie producer), John F. Kennedy (humanitarian/party animal), and Prince Philip, Duke of Edinburgh (gruff, regal *paterfamilias*/sensitive environmentalist). Gemini charms everyone with nonstop talk and fanciful ideas. Gemini rules the lungs (our twin organ) but also the nervous system, which connects all our bodily sensations.

Folklorical significance: Gemini is cross-cultural. Twins are everywhere in prehistory, from Cain and Abel and Romulus and Remus, to Castor and Pollux and Freya and Freyr. This sign also represents the portal—two columns on either side of a door (you can see this in the High Priestess and Justice tarot cards designed by Golden Dawn initiate/artist Pamela Colman Smith). The terrain traditionally associated with Gemini is high and arid—mountains jutting into the sky or locales with landmarks that come in pairs. (This happens more often than you might think—like the two trees growing from the single stump, or the preponderance of binary star systems in the universe versus single stars).

Libra (*September 23 or 24 to October 23 or 24*)

Libra is a cardinal air sign ruled by Venus and represented by the scales. Famous Libras include John Lennon, Franz Liszt, and Sarah Bernhardt. Libras love harmony and partnership, and are frequently indecisive, but oh how charming they can be about it. At least that's what they tell us. And we *want* to believe them, because Libran sincerity is so heartfelt. As for bodily parts, Libra gets the glamorous lumbar region, including ovaries and kidneys.

Folklorical significance: The only object (compared to animal or person) of the zodiac is generally aligned with judicial characters, such as

Justice. Geographic affinities for Libra include (like Gemini) the tops of mountains or hills or buildings; also buildings with dome-shapes built into the architecture, like the Hagia Sophia of Istanbul.

Aquarius (*January 20 or 21 to February 18 or 19*)

Aquarius is a fixed air sign ruled by Uranus. Represented by the water carrier, Aquarians are dreamy, methodical, and humanitarian to an extreme. Ruled by the planet Uranus, Aquarians surprise us all with the unexpected move, but they're usually ahead of the curve. Need investment advice? Call an Aquarian, and find out where the money goes (usually not to them, but that's okay—air signs can swing with that). Famous Aquarians include Lewis Carroll, Virginia Woolf, and Franklin D. Roosevelt. The body parts ruled by Aquarius are seemingly random: the coccyx, and calves and ankles; also the rods and cones in the eyes. Since Aquarius is the water carrier, the veins in the lower leg are also significant for this sign.

Folklorical significance: The strongest association of Aquarius goes back to Ganymede, one of those irresistible mortals Zeus adored. Spirited away to Mount Olympus, the gods gave him the job of cup-bearer—thus Aquarius' representation as a youth pouring water. Locations considered to be Aquarian are landscape features with winding brooks or streams; also natural springs. Since Aquarius rules electricity, locations such as powerhouses, broadcasting stations and studios, and super-highways also fall under his realm.

How to Speak Air Sign

"Huh?" "*Ohmigawsh!*" "Okay, so I was going to do this, and then this person called and then this *other* thing happened . . ." Speaking air sign basically means speeding up your synapses so you're processing and communicating at top speed. Air signs like the open-ended question or ending sentences with a rising inflection so it sounds like a question.

Most air signs are comfortable beginning sentences with "I think," and the really highly evolved ones can add, "So what do *you* think?"

Air signs are the opposite of just-the-facts earth signs. Air signs will tell you the time of day it was, the temperature, where they were, where they were supposed to be, and, then, what? What was I saying? Digressions are an essential part of air sign communication. Hey, it's interesting, right? Believe it or not, meetings overseen by air sign people can be very efficient; they can excel with a schedule in front of them. However, in private, there is very often a tendency to state something, restate it with some variants, mull over what was said, and say it a third time. Getting the message across is something that air signs feel is an infinite exercise. Your earthy pals will say it once (or—worse—mumble, and then wonder why you didn't hear), but air sign people will give you ample opportunity to hear their opinion.

Air signs like to inform: they like to tell you the facts, and they like to express their opinions as if those were facts too. Chances are, your air sign friends have thought more deeply about a topic (in less time) than you. Air signs are adept mimics and enjoy retelling a story in the voice of the person they're talking about.

Being interested in everything is an air sign trait. So is exaggerating or adding superfluous details to a story. For air signs, there is no gossip, it's all just talk. Even so, air signs can respect a confidence as long as you preface your comment by saying something is utterly and *completely off the record.*

Air Sign Parents and Children

Gemini Parents and Children

Divided we stand, divided we fall. Gemini parents can be tons of fun for their kids. Or they're so unpredictable, no one knows where they stand. I've had Gemini clients who had children early and still feel like they need to catch up with their own lives, and Geminis who fulfill nurturing impulses with a wide range of other relationships with neighbors, friends, acquaintances, hobby-pals, and subordinates. Gemini parents can set a great example for their kids by being sociable and showing how easy it is to get on with a variety of people. Geminis can also pick up new learning quickly so they are ideal "homework helpers" as well. Because Gemini rules the lungs, Gemini parents can have a wide range of voices with which to "speak" to their kids. But a warning: if you've got a Gemini child (or you're a Gemini parent who finds consistency a little tiresome), make a point of emphasizing routine and consistency in all your offspring, regardless of sign.

If a child has heavy earth or water elemental influence in his or her chart, he or she can perceive a Gemini parent as being flaky and unreliable. If there's an issue with tardiness, missed deadlines, or incomplete tasks and the Gemini parent can somehow charm their way out of predicaments, this can also have an adverse effect on the kids. Inconsistency can be a hallmark in the day-to-day interaction of Gemini parents, but at their best, these folks can also really imprint their kids with a sense of mission. Judy Garland and Prince Philip (both June 10) each raised their offspring to carry on the family business. Liza Minnelli (March 12) has had the most success of the Garland kids. At the same time, she has unfortunately fought a lengthy and public battle with the family demons of addiction. She's fortunate to live in an era that has far more awareness about such issues than poor Judy's generation ever had.

Of all four Windsor royals, Princess Anne (a Leo, August 15) is said to be the most similar to Gemini Philip. His impatience with procedure, his curiosity about the wider world, and his passion for equestrian sports dovetail with her work ethic and sense of mission.

As for Gemini children—I can't say this to clients enough: regardless of your own Sun sign, your Gemini child is going to want to develop those two personalities. Usually, these amount to angelic/affectionate/verbally nimble and defiant/sulky/impertinent. Gemini kids are very tuned in to characters around them and, as much as they can create enormously complicated worlds of imagination, they are also really sensitive to what others are saying. They're natural mimics and should have a big box of dress-up clothes and hats. They should also be encouraged to have a wide range of friends. These are the kids who are inspired to nurture a wallflower. Gemini doesn't mind being the kid who takes chances and they definitely enjoy being encouraged to act independently.

Libra Parents and Children

Libra as a parent often has the best intentions and then needs extra effort for that follow-through motion. Because Libra is a sign that's all about partnership, Libra is often at their best when in a one-on-one relationship with a child, rather than steering a group. But as a cardinal sign, Libra can be highly protective of their offspring. Libra Sigourney Weaver (October 8) has played a variety of maternal characters, from the chilly mother in *The Ice Storm* to Ellen Ripley in the *Alien* series. She encapsulates a Libra's attitude about motherhood at its forthright best in a 2000 interview she gave to the *Los Angeles Daily News:**

> The great joy about being a parent is that it realigns you totally to care for someone who is not yourself. Before I became a mother, I was basically nurturing myself or my career or my husband, and all of a sudden there's this little person and the rest just seems to fall away, as I think nature intended it to do. You never look at life the same way again.

Libra parents have a strong instinct to be partnered with another and should choose their lifemate with care if they are planning to have kids. Someone will need to make the hard and firm decisions—and someone will need to make sure that consistency happens.

---

* Glenn Whipp, "Super Woman: At 50, Sigourney Weaver Proves It Gets Easier To Do It All," *LA Daily News*, January 25, 2000.

BRINGING OUT THE BEST IN A LIBRA CHILD

Libra children can be all over the map in terms of tractability. All the air signs have a very formative aspect, and the smart parent of a Libra child will emphasize some key concepts:

+ You can do it yourself.
+ It's okay to change your mind, but finish the project anyway.
+ Helping other people get together and get along is a special skill, well within your capabilities.
+ If even your best efforts fail to get others to cooperate, walk away—it's not your failing.
+ (In a store) If you can't make up your mind, get both. Or neither.

Aquarius Parents and Children

Aquarius parents sometimes change gears completely and can be completely dominated by a child with a strong Sun sign. Hands-off parenting can be the result, and Aquarius can put their energy into a cause rather than deal with the nitty-gritty specifics of child-rearing. Aquarius parents are unique in their ability to pick up on aspects of their children the world doesn't see. They'll be responsive to a child who shows a streak of generosity or humanism or a child who has an eccentric interest. Very often, Aquarians don't fully come into their own identity until they have a child. That's when they are compelled to utilize some of the responsible characteristics they've dodged all their lives.

Aquarius children are generally fun, often tractable and easily distracted, but then bizarrely stubborn. Aquarian oldest children can show an outsized sense of authority around the younger ones. They also might be careless with possessions, something that can drive an earth sign parent berserk. Aquarius children are up for adventure and love to be the trendsetter. Don't be surprised or alarmed if an Aquarius kid decides

THE AIR ELEMENT   67

to try out quirky hairdos, makeup schemes, or colorful socks. As a side note, I've known more Aquarius women who have a fetish about ankle socks—remember, Aquarius rules that part of the body.

Keeping your cool with an Aquarius kid who seems to be allergic to follow-through (an air and fire issue), commitment, or staying focused can be a lifelong challenge, especially as the college years loom. It's not unusual for Aquarius to spend some years wandering in the wilderness. Aquarius is also receptive to the idea of a profession that helps a large number of other people or that has a really cool technological focus built in. Aquarius is charming, and one of their traits can be getting taken up by others so that they really don't make a choice about their future so much as drift towards the next interesting opportunity.

This will drive security-minded earth sign parents, or ambitious fire sign parents, or emotionally sensitive water sign parents "right around the bloody bend," as my dad used to say. Aquarius' inconsistency can be the biggest air sign mystery to onlookers, but my experience and observations suggest that Aquarius is always on a unique and unpredictable path. Who would have said that Aquarian Ronald Reagan (February 6) would have migrated out of his show-biz path in his forties on to a far more successful political career? Granted, he was aided, abetted, and encouraged by a highly protective Cancerian wife. No, the best route for the parents of Aquarius kids is to say, "Wow, you made a robot out of styrofoam meat trays, a digital clock, and some soda cans. Can you make another?"

Air Sign Friends and Lovers

Exciting, unpredictable, fun-loving. Air sign lovers are either your cup of tea or one of the more exhausting, frustrating relationships you'll ever try to have. If you *are* an air sign, this probably sounds like an overstatement. You know you're fun and thoroughly devoted—for the time you're devoted. If there ever was an air sign romantic sentiment it's: "If you can't be with the one you love—love the one you're with," as hardheaded Capricorn Stephen Stills (January 3) sang.

Air signs are famously independent and can be an ideal match for someone who doesn't need a lot of emotional care and feeding. Yet two of the three signs—Gemini, signified by the twins and Libra, represented by the scales—would seem to be incomplete without a partner. At least that's what we pick up from their lovable bouts of neediness some of the time.

Air sign people have a wide range of motion, and are often perceived as perennially changeable. Air sign people don't think they're changeable so much as adaptable. Quick responsiveness and fast processing are air sign traits. This can come off as nerviness or flightiness, particularly to a steady-state earth sign person, or an in-touch-with-my-feelings water sign person.

For the most part, air signs are delighted with themselves, once they learn to accept their own inconsistencies and weaknesses. "Choosing one" is sheer torture for an air sign, whether it's dessert, a special outfit, or a trinket. The air sign who knows themselves well will budget enough to get two!

Rather than separate these three kinds of people, let's consider the similarities. Air sign friends can bring a breathless excitement into your life. You'll want them at your parties and your coffee klatch (because they always have gossip, and are always eager to analyze others). They're full of suggestions if you have a problem. Rarely do air signs have that take-no-prisoners single-mindedness more frequently found in fire and earth sign types, but you do want to be flexible if you're befriending a Gemini, Libra, or Aquarius. Or—more accurately—if you find yourself caught up in their slipstream. Both Gemini (ruled by the twins) and Libra (ruled by the balance) can have more enriching one-on-one relationships than Aquarius, even if those relationships are of more brief duration.

All the air signs need plenty of space if you're going to be their friend. Feel free to be vague and open-ended about plans if you need to. They are fine if you don't call them back. If you do make firm plans, however, be sure and send them a reminder call. It's not that they don't want to see you, it's just that in their busy lives, there's always something else worth doing.

Gemini Friends and Lovers

Depending on what else is going on in their chart, air sign lovers can crave stability. The nature of air is to rise above whatever is messy or involved or tiresome or time-consuming. Love relationships for Gemini tend to run long on passion and can be extremely brief, though satisfying. The Mercurial nature of this sign can enhance Gemini's appetite for someone who challenges them or perplexes them. Gems love figuring out puzzles and often there can be a time of life—perhaps the teen years or twenties—when a lover who's completely incomprehensible is the only possible partner!

Doing two things at once is a very Gemini trait. This can include having multiple romantic partners or two groups of friends: those who serve an emotional purpose and those who serve a purely physical purpose.

When I started studying astrology more consistently in the eighties, I noticed that virtually every mass-market astrology book loved to cite the paired example of John F. Kennedy (May 29) and Marilyn Monroe (June 1). At that time, their affair was still a matter of conjecture but their personality traits, the extreme sociability and extroversion, the public personae and clever quips were all stellar examples of Gemini star-power.

Entire books have been written about JFK's wit, wisdom, and ability to deliver an off-the-cuff line. He had great help from Ted Sorensen and other speechwriters, but his ability to roll with the punches and veer from the script has yet to be bettered by a U.S. president. Marilyn's comments and career have prompted an entire realm of feminist studies since her 1962 death. Seeing both sides of the world was one of her gifts as an interviewee. Consider the following: "Hollywood is a place where they'll pay you a thousand dollars for a kiss and fifty cents for your soul." Or "I'm a failure as a woman. My men expect so much of me, because of the image they've made of me and that I've made of myself, as a sex symbol. Men expect so much and I can't live up to it."

One can as easily picture JFK in a suit as in casual sports clothes. He was the first president seen in full relaxation mode as well as chief-executive armor and the public loved it. (No, Ike's golfing pictures didn't have the same impact.) As for Marilyn, her most lasting images are those showing her in couture finery—or nude.

I bring up these two superstars because it's important for those who love, adore, and mate with Gemini to understand what you're dealing with. If your easygoing Gem gets irritated at slow service in a restaurant, or seems hypersensitive to others' moods, your best strategy is to acknowledge their mood change and admit that you are not bothered by whatever is bugging them. The Mercurial side of Gemini sometimes craves constant stimulation and often has a difficult time kicking back. A Gemini who can do a yoga class—and love it—is a highly evolved animal. In my experience, a Gemini who will do kick-boxing this month, jazz dance next month, and suddenly show an interest in horseback riding is more typical of the breed.

Gemini friends can be the perfect companion for seeing a play or attending a lecture. Even better is visiting a museum, attending an arts and crafts fair, or going to the carnival. The theme is any activity where you want to discuss what you're expriencing. As Gemini rules the lungs, you can find them to be chatterboxes when it's not appropriate, and any excursion that requires walking and talking (shopping?) can be great fun for them.

To keep a Gemini as a lover, it's best to roll with the punches as best you can. Gemini doesn't like being called on inconsistency (for the most part), and the smart lover will learn when to listen and when to tune out the chatter.

Libra Friends and Lovers

The seventh sign of the zodiac rules partnership, and the uncoupled Libra is a rare beast indeed. In my practice I've had lifelong independent, free-spirit, don't-need-no-one Aquarians, and Geminis who get that three's-a-crowd feeling whenever they're involved with someone. With Libra, the urge to merge is intense but so is their tendency towards self-doubt once they're actually in a relationship. The air signs really can mesh with virtually any other element. Some Libras only learn who they are by being in a relationship, so you'll find scales people involved with a wide variety of personality types: shy, outgoing, thoughtful, careless, scheming, dreaming, you get the idea. Some Libras so ache to form a permanent connection with another that they'll put up with inordinate amounts of bad behavior from a partner.

The number of Libras who get involved with strong and egotistical mates is pretty impressive, yet one must ask oneself—what's in it for Libra? In many cases, stability and an identity. A graceful, cautious Libra with a partner who'll say any old darn thing is a Libra who gets to avoid direct confrontation. Don't be misled by that harmony-seeking aspect of Libra. They really do have a sense of perspective and some will behave in a willful or controversial manner (Eminem, October 17; *American Idol*'s Simon Cowell, October 7). The lightning rod Libras are often so charming and/or charismatic, it's easy to forgive their transgressions.

The charm very often comes with a genuine humor, if not bemusement at how the world works. When I started researching famous Libra performers, what struck me was how few of them play the tragedienne, and how often they specialize in lighter, more farcical roles. They may have the looks of a goddess or serious dramatic actor, but usually make their mark in comedy.

Consider the careers of the following funny ladies: Madeline Kahn (September 29), Fran Drescher (September 30), Julie Andrews (October 1), Alicia Silverstone (October 4), Carole Lombard (October 6), Joan Cusack (October 11), Penny Marshall (October 15), Suzanne Somers (October 16), Pam Dawber (October 18), even Margaret Dumont (October 20, see "Matchups, Libra and Libra") and Annette Funicello (October 22). All these women are noted for comedy and a certain light touch: they can do melodrama and even tragedy, but that's not how the public wants to see them. And is there anyone on that list you wouldn't mind as a casual friend?

The best-adjusted Libra lover will be tolerant, not easily ruffled, and able to deal with whatever comes along. Libra usually has a hard time maintaining intense feelings, since those scales need to keep tipping. Some fickleness early in life isn't totally out of place with this sign and they're one of the few who can maintain intense intimacy with one person while having a need to be part of the crowd at the same time. The anchorite tendencies of their fellow cardinal signs, Capricorn and Cancer, are totally antithetical to this sign. Libra friends can be less susceptible to the flavor-of-the-month fickleness of charming Gemini. Libra can also be occasionally shy or recessive, waiting to see what you suggest. Their favorite word, "whatever," can either be music to your ears (if you like to take the lead), or a slow drip from a leaky faucet into your sink of tolerance. Should enough droplets accumulate in the basin, you might want to tear out your hair.

If you're the Libra and wondering who your best partner is, know this: of all the signs, you have the greatest flexibility. You may be drawn to muscular and decisive, or sensitive and frail, or something in between, but my advice is to wander the food court of love and friendship: spend time with a variety of personalities but always stick with someone who makes you laugh and whom you can make laugh as well.

I was once backstage in a club in Boston after a Jerry Lee Lewis (September 29) performance. His (fifth, I believe) wife at the time was by his side, looking nervously at all the female visitors who came through. Jerry Lee was a fireplug of a man, and in repose had a malevolent, mischief-making aura. You could tell he was used to being deferred to, yet he had the affect of someone constantly looking for a fight. At one point, he looked at each of the women in the room and pointed his finger. "You're a nice girl, you're a nice girl, you're *not* a nice girl, you're a nice girl," he said. Unfortunately, he never explained exactly what he meant by "nice," but with his being a fellow raised in the courtly South, I can only assume he was gauging who would be quick with the bread-and-butter note after dinner. Anyway, it was a memorable example of Libra decision making!

When I was first learning about astrology, I was perplexed that only one sign of the twelve was an object and not an animal or person. Now I have a greater appreciation for the fact that the "thing" is actually a potent and symbolic psychological representative. The scales are always pictured in balance but for many Libras, achieving that balanced feeling can be a daily struggle.

Thus the tendency towards codependency. Some Libras can manifest a chameleonic affect so that they mysteriously "fit" with their partners. Rock star Sting (October 2) has made a fetish out of his physical relationship with wife Trudie Styler—yet has no problem playing the Pan-like rock 'n' roll sex god to the greater public. And Gore Vidal (October 3), that brilliant and grumpy expatriate, was never more famous than when he was feuding with Norman Mailer and Truman Capote. Without someone to spar with, to play against, to react to, sometimes Libra is a little lost—or wants us to look at them that way. So, we take a step nearer and ask "Are you okay?" and are greeted with the warmest of smiles.

Aquarius Friends and Lovers

The Aquarius lover is idealistic and extremely subtle about exhibiting neediness. Yet their passions run deep and they can definitely mate for life. With their Uranian ruler, Aquarians are comfortable with surprises and the unexpected twist or change of plans. Aquarius can be as prone to the obsessive relationship as the next person, but what sets them apart is their ability to change direction at a moment's notice.

Like the other air signs, Aquarius lovers generally don't have a type. You'll find them mated with fire, air, earth, and water and perfectly content as long as they don't perceive their lover to be unduly possessive. Yes, that's what I mean to say: I've seen Aquarians with highly protective, engaged companions, but as long as the Aquarius is oblivious, all is well in their world.

Commitment can be the unthinkable concept to many young Aquarians. Their questing, curious nature can keep them in a constant state of distraction. Getting attracted to someone and then feeling obsessed can put them in a panic. A happy Aquarius lover will bring wild ideas and outlandish entertainment notions to a companion. "Let's try this restaurant, let's visit this new place, let's go to this party, and yes, I only know the host."

Aquarius is notorious for talking about what will happen next—not what is happening now. If Aquarius ends up with an earth sign or Cancer, their partner will need to learn how to let them dream out loud. Practicalities are usually the last item on their to-do list. If you want to keep an Aquarius lover, give them a long leash, and a calendar with all kinds of interesting events penciled in for the coming weeks. Penciled? Absolutely. Aquarius is one of those signs that lives in the future, but when the present intervenes, it's a big bummer.

Aquarius friends can be adventure-hounds. Suggest the out-of-the-way café in the iffy section of town, or the late-night pub crawl, or the impromptu road trip, and you might get a cock of the head and then, "Sure, I've got nothing else planned," even if they had something else planned. Aquarius can also be the leader of such an excursion, and if you're not able to attend, it's no big deal; they'll just move on to the next person in their collection.

WHY EVERYONE NEEDS AN AQUARIAN FRIEND

+ Because the tribal love rock musical *Hair* told us it was the Age of Aquarius.

+ Because if you're going to get in a negative frame of mind about something, they'll give you a little bit of time to vent, and fixate, and then insist you change the topic.

+ Because they set such a great example of how to move on when it's time.

+ Because you can always give them a valentine-themed birthday present and they won't misinterpret your intentions.

+ Because they don't go crazy if you forget to call.

WHY EVERYONE NEEDS AN AQUARIAN LOVER (AT LEAST ONCE)

+ Because when I canvassed the folks I know (clients, family, etc.), Aquarius was the sign that came up most frequently as an agreeable romantic companion—and I asked representatives of all twelve signs!

+ Because they'll appreciate you at your quirkiest and most honest.

+ Because they're not possessive, so when they're really into you, you'll feel like you've accomplished something extraordinary.

+ Because they don't go crazy if you forget to call.

Air Sign Preoccupations, Obsessions, and Addictions

Air signs can have classic tastes just as easily as they can be crazy about trends. They can be materialistic (Libra), or happy to give their things away as it makes room for something new (Aquarius, Gemini). I've known more air sign women who (like their water-sign sisters) are always up on the latest self-help trend book. Obsessions for air signs tend to be short-lived, although for some signs, finding something they like, whether it's a particular brand of jeans, a band, or a breed of dog can provoke the same kind of loyalty you'd find in an earth sign.

Air signs are capable of sentimentality, but never to the extent of an earth or water sign person. I bet you know plenty of air sign people or those with a preponderance of air in their charts who can process conversations, interactions, and activities more quickly than the next person. These are the individuals who help us move along as they have a tendency not to linger over experiences or live in the past. Sure, they can have long memories and carry a grudge but they can also focus on something coming up.

Books, computer programs and games, interesting one-function tools, or cooking implements can be things air signs like to have around them. Anything that provides information is also key. When Google first came out, the people I know who instantly figured out all the Easter egg features beyond simple searching were air signs (and one canny Scorpio). Air signs also enjoy streamlining their filing systems, and miniature or sample versions of products (to save getting bored with a fragrance, skin cream, or shampoo).

Air Sign Work and Careers: Choosing a Career That Will Fuel Your Soul

Air signs are great at communicating, and can gather, analyze, and disseminate information quickly. They can be at their best communicating to groups because they'll instantly understand how to present information in a variety of manners to suit every learner.

Despite their sociability and ease in group situations, many of them, at some point, choose a career that requires periods of solitude and reflection, and separation from the masses. Part of the innate flexibility of this element is to keep things interesting for themselves. Every time an air sign gets an entry-level job as an administrative assistant, answering phones and connecting others, they'll need corresponding intervals in a room of their own to balance things out.

Air sign workers can be commendably devoted and loyal on the job, as long as they feel they're effective and that others are working at the same high frequency. Woe betide the sluggish coworker of an air sign who lets the files pile up, or who doesn't answer phone calls right away. Interestingly, what I've found in workplaces is that you can have a pile of earth sign workers who function well, or a collection of water sign people, and even a workplace where there are some fire sign folks who work together. With air signs, however, it seems they are generally a one-of-a-kind in their work environment. Maybe that's because too much would get done if there were lots working together.

Gemini Careers, Coworkers, and Bosses

Like Virgo, Gemini is ruled by Mercury. This predisposes them towards jobs that utilize Mercurial values and qualities. "Here's a new idea; I came up with it this morning" is a classic Gemini gambit on the job.

Gemini rules the third house of peers, siblings, short messages, and travels. A career that includes many brief encounters could be thoroughly fulfilling as well as jobs that enable Gemini to have short but intense one-on-one relationships. Work that puts them in brief contact with lots of others is satisfying to them; they don't need long and involved relationships on the job to feel effective. Their biggest demon as an employee is getting bored—also true of Aquarius.

Working in an educational environment (e.g., school, university, institute), marketing/promotions, or database management would be satisfactory. Couples counseling, working in media and reporting, or sales (especially with short sales trips) could be a great fit. So could selling an item that has frequent upgrades or changes of design. The bottom line is that Gemini will always have a job that has "communication with others" as an essential part of the activity.

Geminis can blend well into any workplace and are often the go-to people when someone new arrives. They can suss out useful information, from where the copy machine toner is kept and how to install it, to which nearby restaurant has the best lunch specials. Gemini can be an excellent on-the-job trainer for others; they pick up new skills quickly themselves.

In the 1950s, actor Clint Eastwood (May 31) didn't stand out in the pack of hunky Hollywood leading men, but when he collaborated with Italian filmmaker Sergio Leone in the 1960s, his minimalist acting style came into its own. Eastwood quickly picked up the complicated skills of filmmaking—from setting up shots to lighting, to creating a soundtrack, and has basically written his own ticket as a multi-talented, multitasking creator ever since.

Laurie Anderson (June 5) has enjoyed a classically divided crossover career. In the late 1970s, she was an avant-garde artist who experimented with myriad electronic effects on her violin as well as her voice; she had an unexpected pop hit with the 1981 single, "O Superman." Her concerts are one of the few places where the symphony crowd mixes with the gallery-goers and pop music fanciers.

Gemini workers have a built-in advantage in that they can be excellent collaborators as well as project leaders, such as Francis Crick (June 8), or South African playwright Athol Fugard (June 11), who wrote many of his plays in collaboration with great South African actors such as John Kani and Winston Ntshona. World-traveling conceptual artist Christo (June 13) is indebted to his wife, Jeanne-Claude, who helps manage his projects. Even sexpert advisor Xaviera Hollander (June 15) has had a long and productive publishing relationship with the *Playboy* magazine company.

Gemini bosses can be fun and erratic, and the smart ones will surround themselves with earth signs to get things done, water signs to smooth the way, and fire and air signs for brainstorming. Gemini supervisors can be outrageously informal one moment and then bound to protocol the next. If you're a delicate sort, and you find yourself trying to second-guess your Gemini boss, it may be time to think about a transfer. You will never be able to out-strategize them.

Libra Careers, Coworkers, and Bosses

Libra jobs and careers can fall under the super-aesthetic: interior design, fashion, jewelry, decorating, beauty trade, skin care, and other personal improvement lines of work. Making the world more beautiful is a Libra mission, which can include adding harmony to music. All the air signs can and should be good at communications, so media and marketing, journalism and broadcasting, writing, lecturing, and researching are all useful Libra occupations.

Libra rules the seventh house of partnerships and relationships, so they very often develop one close friendship in their work environment. With Venus as their ruling planet, presenting themselves well on the job really matters to them. These are the folks you want to ask to pick out the birthday card for the office-mate or wrap the present.

The Libra employee wants to learn the rules, get along, understand the group dynamic, and be appreciated. That Venus rulership also enhances Libra's ability to walk into a workplace and immediately strike everyone as a pleasant personality and a good listener. All of a sudden, others are going to Libra with grievances, concerns about projects that are going off-track, or other workplace issues. If the Libra is just one of the gang, they may find themselves fueling dissatisfaction by echoing others' sentiments about poor decisions being made. You can always trust Libra to see both sides, which can make them effective when dealing with negotiations or other interactions among groups with different goals.

Your Libra coworker can be several steps ahead of you. And if they are—it makes them uncomfortable. In meeting situations, they're quick with this kind of preamble: "Let me play devil's advocate for a moment here," or "Another consideration we really need to think about is . . ." Please understand that Libra doesn't necessarily have a preference, or even a point of view. They have *all* points of view and will be more comfortable if everyone else can acknowledge the myriad facets of any proposed endeavor.

If you are partners with a Libra—equal partners—you're in luck. At their best, they will be scrupulous about shared responsibilities, and they'll be very happy to have things spelled out. If it's their responsibility to be the point of contact with outside clients or others, be assured they'll represent your business fairly and accurately. And they'll also make an effort to be put-together when they meet with the public.

Libra

Your birthday always comes during that period when everyone is finally getting into the groove for school. Though it's
harvest time, you don't always feel like reaping the rewards
of work done during the spring and summer just yet. During your birthday weeks, you feel there's always more to do—
more to improve on. Other times this is the case include late
May and June, and late January and February (just as the
days are getting longer). Times when you could be forced
into making a decision (that's the correct decision, yet makes
you nervous) include late March through mid-April, late
June through mid-July, and Christmas through late January.

Libra can be the boss, though this isn't the most natural fit for them,
certainly not in their younger years. Libra needs to learn how to lead,
and they can learn a lot if they work with and for Aries, Capricorn,
and even Cancers. If they work their way up to being in charge, it can
be highly uncomfortable for them to be in a position of giving orders
versus making suggestions. You'd be amazed how quickly they can
turn once they have some authority, however. If Libra comes in from
the outside, they will probably spend some time getting to know the
people in the work environment, and seeing whether people are well-
suited (temperamentally and experience-wise) to their tasks.

The worst scenario with a Libra boss is one who abdicates completely, encouraging workers to figure out their own path. They may
then come charging in at the eleventh hour asking, "Why was *this* decision made?" If you work with a Libra boss, you will definitely curry favor by using the phrase "on the other hand," stating your case, and *then*

expressing a clear preference if pushed. Remember: saving a Libra from making a decision is a smart move.

Aquarius Career, Coworkers, and Bosses

Everyone works with an Aquarius at some point. This fixed air sign is not driven by the same concerns for security as are the other signs, and these folks are often curious about trying new things. Aquarius prevails over the eleventh house of hopes, wishes, dreams, friendship, mass movements, and trends. Uranus, which governs surprises, electricity, and kinetic energy is the ruling planet. A job that would anticipate or reflect trends, such as market research or any kind of polling, would be of interest. So would jobs that deal with electricity, such as engineering, electric repairs, lighting designer, computer programmer or designer, or broadcaster or broadcast technician. In a conventional field, such as health care or corporate activity, they'll always be curious about alternative paths: herbs for the nurse, seminars that combine business with philosophy for the executive.

Humanitarian interests can also be an Aquarian pursuit, albeit one that may take years of effort. Some Aquarians do a job they love, and end up being real pacesetters with a lasting influence on the world. Dancer Anna Pavlova (January 31), musician Bob Marley (February 6), and author Laura Ingalls Wilder (February 7) were pursuing careers that they loved, unaware their work would be beloved by generations yet to be born.

Aquarius also has a rebel side. You can always count on your Aquarian coworker to point out inequities (once they notice them) or to wonder exactly what the working conditions are in the factory your business is dealing with. They are less concerned about getting theirs and are more concerned about everyone being cared for. If, however, they suspect they're being asked to do something outside their realm, and, in actuality, someone *else's* charge, there will be protestations.

Aquarius doesn't mind changing careers several times. They can train for some specific task, and as soon as they're certified, realize they need a break. Because air signs are social and Aquarius is technical, you can find them in various customer-service situations. They can anticipate others' needs because of their quick-wittedness (versus Cancer's ability to absorb and interpret emotional cues). If they're in sales, they'll be the ones delighted to go on cold calls no matter how nervous they tell you they are.

Aquarius bosses can be deflected from the business at hand, which they'd just as soon leave to the bean counters, and are delighted to talk about what's coming up. Excellent Aquarian bosses trust the people working for them and understand the importance of delegating but they're also extremely malleable; you may find that they say one thing one week, and the next week the entire plan has changed.

Unlike Leo, their astrological opposite, they rarely have an investment in pomp, circumstance, or trappings of any particular position, and they're much more persuadable. If you want to get ahead around your Aquarian boss, use phrases like "new," "exciting," "getting everyone on board," "attracting a wider audience," and "trend-setting in a good way."

four

THE WATER ELEMENT

Introduction

Lovable and maddening, the water signs surge through the zodiac, gliding over rough obstacles and flowing around corners . . . most of the time, that is. This final element in the fire, earth, air, water pattern is traditionally interpreted as the sensing, feeling, perceiving membership of the twelve signs, and much of the time this is true. However, water signs can be as impulsive as fire signs, stubborn as earth signs, and scattered as air signs—depending on how they *feel* and what they *perceive*, of course.

Water signs can be difficult to read. You can look at their faces and think you're seeing excitement, when what's actually on view is irritation. Sometimes you think they're not reacting at all, and in fact they're in raptures. All the water signs come with a built-in self-protection device that can range from turning the tables (Cancer's habit of responding to "How are you?" with "Oh, how are *you*?") to darkly droll humor

(Pisces and Scorpio, the former of which can actually laugh at themselves. Later. Much later.)

But water signs—like the element—can go anywhere and penetrate even the most firmly trodden ground. Really well-evolved water signs understand they're sensitive, accept their deep feelings, and learn to cope. Coping mechanisms for water signs often involve time apart from others. These folks are social, but they also need to recharge and zone out.

A Brief Overview of the Water Signs

The traits that water signs can share include artistic ability and/or appreciation, plus sensitivity and perceptiveness. Aside from that, these three can be as different as chalk and cheese. Water signs can also have some very odd effects on one another. People with a lot of water in their charts can be natural confidantes who have great listening skills. Which is different from being able to provide great feedback, although they'll definitely sympathize with you if it seems you're enduring an injustice.

Cancer (June 22 or 23 to July 22 or 23)

Cancer is a cardinal water sign ruled by the Moon. It rules the fourth house, whose domain is home and personal security. Represented by the crab, Cancers can be home-loving, deeply domestic, fiercely loyal and self-protective, and prone to stomach upsets when life doesn't go their way. Cancers feel everything very deeply, but won't necessarily tell. Well, they will, but on their time. They prefer to move sideways—frequently. Cancer rules the stomach, but also has been assigned the breasts and chest, plus pancreas. Henry David Thoreau (July 12) was a Cancer, and a quirky version of the breed. Famous for his cabin at Walden, a home he describes in builder's detail in his most famous book, he basically turned the entire outside world into an extension of his inner landscape. He showed that wandering tendency that many crabs have in early life, making extensive journeys to Maine, Cape Cod, and parts of New England that were still wilderness in the nineteenth century.

Folklorical significance: Cancer goes back to the Egyptians, whose pictorial interpretation of the sign was the scarab beetle, another arthropod. The constellation of Cancer is invisible during the longest day of the year, so in the Northern Hemisphere it is actually the least-visible sign. But elsewhere in the world, you'll see it on or around June 21. Like the namesake crab, the Sun during this period remains high in the sky for a few days then appears to start moving backward towards the south. Cancerian locations would be aquatic: lakes and ponds more likely than fast-moving streams. In your home, the kitchen is the natural place of Cancer, as the sign rules bakers (also masseurs).

Scorpio (October 24 or 25 to November 22 or 23)

Scorpio is a fixed water sign formerly ruled by Mars, now by Pluto (which astrologers still consider a planet, *thankyouverymuch*), represented by the scorpion. Famous Scorpios include Prince Charles, Picasso, Robert F. Kennedy, and Hillary Clinton. Scorps mystify more people than any other sign, mostly because the themes of sex, death, and other people's money rule the eighth house, Scorpio's natural home. Charming but not overly sociable, your typical Scorps are charismatic and occasionally devious with an ethical compass all their own. Scorpio's domain is the reproductive system and the elimination system. This includes bladder, urethra, prostate, groin, rectum, all sexual organs and—interestingly enough—the nostrils. I've known some Scorpios who are intensely sensitive to smells, and attracted to the most surprising odors.

Folklorical significance: Artemis, the virgin Moon goddess and older sister of Apollo (the Sun god), was known for her prowess in hunting. Orion the hunter boasted that he had the best skills and could hunt any beast in the wilderness. He made the mistake of bragging directly to Artemis and her mother, the nymph Leto. This is what's known as *hubris*—pride before the gods—one of Scorpio's possible downfalls.

Gaia (Mother Earth) got wind of Orion's bragging and conjured up a gigantic scorpion. You can almost see her muttering in the workroom, "Hunt *this*, you arrogant mortal!" Orion got more than he bargained for, for sure. A huge battle took place and though he killed the scorpion, it managed to sting him fatally. The happy ending is that Zeus, great admirer of all crazy challenges, took each combatant and placed them in the sky but at a very great distance from one another. That's why you will never see these two constellations at the same time: Scorpio rises only after Orion sets. Scorpio's constellation includes the star Antares ("against Aries" i.e., a half-year away). Scorpionic locations are watery, but not exactly vacation spots: hidden places where wastewater drains, like bogs and swamps. Compost heaps are Scorpionic so if you want to thrill your green-thumb Scorpio, set up a little bucket for them to dump coffee grounds and fruit peels.

Pisces (February 19 or 20 to March 20 or 21)

Pisces is a mutable water sign ruled by Neptune. Represented by two fish swimming in opposite directions, some Pisces, like some Libras, thrive in indecision, especially of the emotional-quandary type. Pisces rules the twelfth house, which is the place in the zodiac where everything that didn't fit in the first eleven houses goes. Their themes include the subconscious, hiding places, prisons, x-rays, secrets, and backstage in theaters. Places the public doesn't go to are very attractive to Pisces, which is why some of them are most happy when working behind the scenes (this is true of all watery folks to some degree, but Pisces can make a career of it). Sometimes they'll take the spotlight and, when they do, they'll be inimitable, memorable, and slightly strange (Karen Carpenter and Lou Reed are both Pisces).

The parts of the body considered Pisces' areas are the feet and toes. Thus people with a heavy Pisces influence can have a shoe fetish. (When planets move through the sign of Pisces, you may find your desire for footwear is enhanced!) Consider that interval between the end of winter and the beginning of the warm weather, when the sun moves into Pisces. Once those snow boots are off, don't we all feel like getting new shoes?

Folklorical significance: Pisces goes all the way back to Babylon. Typical Piscean places include the deep ocean and locations where serious fishing happens. Unlike Cancer (aquatic, but near the confluence of land and water) and Scorpio (scorpions are desert creatures for heck's sake), Pisces gets the world's seas and vertical miles of water. Land areas for this sign include oil tanks, places that have flooded, evangelical churches, plus anywhere a séance happens.

How to Speak Water Sign

"Are you okay?" "I feel so . . ." "What will people think?" "And how did that make *you* feel?" "That sounds really difficult—one time that happened to me . . ." Speaking water sign means being either over-the-top empathetic or somehow translating other people's experiences into your own story. Basically, the best way to communicate with water sign folks is just to be patient and still. They're hypersensitive to listening abilities and you will not be able to fool them if you're not completely invested in what they're saying.

Unlike air or fire signs, water signs will expect you to weigh in with your take on things. They can also presume that experiences are more difficult or challenging than you might find them. This is a very, very useful skill, and I've known plenty of water sign folks who are in the position of listener, whether this means being a pastor, therapist, teacher, editor, or translator. Water signs can hear something and then communicate a clear version to the rest of the world. One of the advantages of being in touch with one's own feelings is that you can be in touch with everyone else's feelings too. Water signs who are hypersensitive definitely need to have friends who are slightly less well adjusted. Having unfortunates to look out for makes life easier for many water signs who otherwise might focus inward, on their own feelings.

That listening aspect can actually have a downside. Depending on the personal chemistry, you might know a water sign person to whom you are constantly saying, "Oh, it wasn't so bad," or "I'll get over it," because of an overactive sympathy gland on their part. Sometimes this can take the form of the water sign person getting indignant on *your* behalf because you are failing to respond as they would. Being able to get over trifles and small setbacks is a sign of maturity, and the best-natured water signs have a very go-with-the-flow attitude that makes them attractive to everyone.

Water Sign Parents and Children

Loving and distracted and sensitive and caring and sentimental. Very sentimental. Water sign parents often take great pleasure in raising children and delight in their little quirks and comments and actions. But there's also a level of distractedness that can set in; water signs can be the dreamers of the zodiac.

Water sign parents are interested in how their kids feel . . . about everything. This can translate into a surprising permissiveness. The fixed and cardinal water signs (Scorpio and Cancer) are better disposed to be consistent about child-rearing techniques. Water signs are excellent at promoting their child's creativity and most of them will also see the value of early socialization. Water sign parents are sensitive to sniffles, coughs, and allergies. They're more likely to feel their child's pain when the child may have one of life's setbacks (a broken friendship, a strike-out at the bat). Water sign children are much more sensitive than you think they are and they also have long memories. They can be encouraged to express themselves in every possible medium: physical activity, visually, and artistically through performance or music.

Cancer Parents and Children

That Moon rulership can make for a very loving, very involved parent. Since Cancer rules the home, a Cancer parent is highly sensitive to cozy, comfortable surroundings. Lots of pillows, couches, and chairs you can sink into—those are the surroundings Cancer wants for their family. Cancer also has no patience for that old adage: nature or nurture. It's nurture all the way! Protective and loyal, Cancer will support their children in friendships they deem appropriate and they are passionately interested in what their children are thinking or feeling.

Overprotective? Cancer parents can be. The other, more unusual and rare side of Cancerian parenting is a deliberate signing-off on offspring behavior and choices. Sometimes Cancer has an easier time when the kids are small versus when the kids are bigger, starting to make their own choices.

As for Cancer children—you'll be amazed at how sensitive they are and how early it comes for them. If there's some downtrodden little child in their class, the loneliness will bother them even if they don't extend a hand of friendship immediately. Cancer children are highly perceptive, tougher than you think, sentimental, and capable of feats of leadership that can startle others. Their identity in a group very often is the little mother or caretaker. When I have clients with Cancer children, or who are expecting a baby in late June or July, I always advise them to purchase a tiny baking set and be prepared to spend a lot of time playing with clay and other plastic materials. That impulse to knead isn't confined to just pussycats!

If you are a parent of a Cancer child reading this, you could be thinking, "But my child is *so* sensitive and emotional. They'll be fine for a while and then some trivial event will push them over the edge. What do I do?" As with all water signs, the need to process emotional events is strong. And once they vent, they're usually done. It's when they *don't* vent that you have problems.

Cancer kids can play on a team perfectly happily, and they can also be excellent cheerleaders for others, especially those lacking their natural talents or abilities. However, there is a huge disparity between the genders with Cancer. The females can be steady and consistent, while the males can develop a hyperactive defensive side. I think this is because Cancer males' natural domestic impulses are so often thwarted by conflicting gender-role expectations.

Scorpio Parents and Children

Scorpio is highly protective and understands the importance of routine and consistency, meanwhile claiming the right to subvert routine and consistency if they so choose! Scorpio has a great fondness for growing things, despite that Pluto rulership; Scorpio parents can be very tough-minded with their kids and the world.

Scorpio parents do expect a certain degree of independence from their kids. I've known some Scorpio parents whose kids get into trouble and the general response is, "The door is always open, but you need to start making the right choice." The autocratic side that comes with Cancer (albeit in a passive-aggressive package) is largely absent with Scorpio.

Nevertheless, do not expect a completely *laissez-faire* attitude towards parenting from your Scorpio buddies. Remember: they know how to strategize. So they like to know what their kids are doing, who they're with, and when they'll be back. They're canny enough to do this in a relaxed but firm manner.

Consider the fate of the Grimaldi children after the death of Monaco's Princess Grace (November 12): While the princess was alive, the three children were kept on a fairly tight leash (despite Princess Caroline's early and ill-advised first marriage, later annulled). After Princess Grace perished in a car crash, the youngest child, Princess Stephanie, deliberately went on an unregal path designing swimsuits, cranking out pop records, and having a collection of children out of wedlock. Both Stephanie and Caroline are free-spirited Aquarians, but it's still difficult to imagine Princess Grace's daughter recording heavy-breathing electronic Eurodisco had the princess lived. As for us commoners, Scorpio moms and dads can be protective and have to be mindful to give their kids some freedom.

Scorpio children are big on "why" and "how come," and are generally tough little customers. They don't like to back down from a point of view, and will seem to be emotionally self-sufficient years before they actually are. Having them develop a hobby or area of expertise will go a long way towards helping a little scorpion feel fulfilled. The wise parent will try out a variety of activities, including solitary ones like art and craft classes, so that their child can achieve mastery. Scorpio can be a team player, but on their own terms. If you're looking for a role for your little boy or girl on the team, go for defense.

Pisces Parents and Children

The natural instinct for water sign folks is to take care of others. Pisces parents are no different from Cancer or Scorpio when it comes to feeling protective of their little ones. Fishie fathers and mothers, however, can also let down their guard more than the other two water signs. If they have a child with strong fire or earth influence, they can easily be manipulated. Pisces parents have to be careful that they show consistency with their children. With a tendency to be distracted, setting limits and boundaries will be a struggle for them and one that can take its toll emotionally. In a Pisces/other sign parenting relationship, the Pisces will usually be happy for someone else to be the enforcer. On the brighter side, Pisces can encourage and support their children to a degree that other parents wouldn't.

Pisces can also subordinate their relationship with their child to a relationship with a partner—which can be emotionally problematic if the children are still at an impressionable age (this is unthinkable for Cancer, and not on the radar for Scorpio). For a Pisces parent to thrive, they don't necessarily have to work outside the home, but they do need to feel as though they are providing a safe and comfortable "home base" for offspring.

Like Capricorn kids, Pisces little ones can seem older than their years in some regards. They can be the ones who seem to know when people are hurting. They'll stay up late with a parent while waiting for the wild older brother or sister to come home. However, there can be an emotional cost with this kind of empathy.

Because Pisces are so concerned about others' feelings, they often neglect their own. More than any other sign, they can get into a people-pleasing mode. If you're the parent of a Pisces child, try to avoid making their decisions for them. "Do you want peas or carrots" is better than "Do you want peas or carrots? I know you like carrots so much, so that's why I made them for you." Pisces is highly sensitive to others doing them favors and they will want to avoid confrontation *and* make you happy.

Also, Pisces kids often come with natural talents, usually artistic or musical. The wise parent will provide opportunities for Pisces to explore a particular medium and get them socialized as early as possible. It is very helpful for them to see how other people interact. They also need to see that people can get angry—on their own or at someone else—and then work it out and move on.

Pisces can bottle up emotions to the point where they need an outlet, and I've had plenty of Pisces clients who either have a weakness for substance abuse or a weakness for others who have a substance abuse problem! Little fish are not going to be the tough or insensitive kid—

they'll be the brooder and the thoughtful one. They also need a time to recharge, and they can get very involved in fantasy role-playing games or other forms of escapism. This is absolutely normal and natural and should be allowed.

Water Sign Friends and Lovers

For the most part, you've hit the jackpot when it comes to someone who has fully functioning emotional development. Water sign lovers can be attentive, romantic, thoughtful, tender, sensitive to one's needs and desires, and fun-loving in the sack. They can also be possessive, moody, unpredictable, hypersensitive to slights, and capable of unpredictable mood shifts to the degree that you wonder *what* set them off.

Water sign lovers enjoy the process of intimacy, the build-up, the experience of the date, sharing a significant experience together, whether it's a concert, weepy movie, or art exhibition. Water sign lovers can also have no sense of time and be lacking time-management skills, so tardiness can be an issue.

Water sign people seek a soul mate, but can also spend long periods of time on their own between partnerships. This is not time that they mourn—rather, they understand better than any other sign the importance of recharging.

Cancer Friends and Lovers

Fiercely loyal and fascinated by others' motivations, a Cancer lover is someone you'll probably have to woo. They are highly self-protective, but if you catch them at a vulnerable time *and* show that you are to be trusted, they're absolutely, unequivocally yours.

Because Cancer rules the fourth house—the home—a Cancer might go through periods of being on the town pretty constantly, but the time invariably comes when they cocoon—big time. And no one can cocoon like a hard-shelled arthropod. Thus you'll always find comfy cushions at a Cancer's home—chairs where you can stretch out, big couches you can disappear into. Cancer likes comfort, and an ideal piece of furniture for them would be matching lounge chairs, to share with that special someone.

Cancer also rules the stomach—which means the kitchen is key. I've never had a client who was a Cancer who didn't tell me they were happiest bustling in the kitchen, cooking up a romantic meal for a lover. If you're dating a Cancer, you can bowl them over with cooking skills. And if you lack those, they will be highly appreciative of your awe and gratitude for the meal *they* cook.

Cancer likes security and they can also be grateful for routines. If you're their loved one, you can add to their feelings of security by being reliable about calling when you say you will. If you don't say you'll call—they won't expect it. But the minute you set up an expectation is the minute you invest (in their worldview).

Cancer lovers are usually pretty up-front about how their childhood has operated in their life, and if you are embarking on a relationship with a crab, be patient if they need to air stories of small grievances or early events. They are in a constant process of self-evaluation and understanding, and the thoughtful lover will give them space to do so.

But the range of motion exhibited by crabs is fairly awesome, and one of my favorite ménages to analyze in astrology classes is what I call "The Cancer Paradox"—Princess Diana and Camilla Shand Parker Bowles Windsor. Now if we know two things about Scorpio Prince Charles, it's that he likes blondes and Cancers, preferably in the same package. His first, and clearly most enduring, love was with Camilla Shand (July 17). Camilla's Cancerian virtues are, first and foremost, extreme loyalty.

Diana Spencer (July 1) had the sign's private impulses for the first two-thirds of her life. Even her childhood pictures show a shy personality, and once she began dating Prince Charles, the tabloid images of her were uniform in depicting a pretty girl with lowered head, gazing at her own shoes.

Camilla has never been shy, but then, she came from a less-damaged family background. Diana's parents' early divorce and subsequent court battles (Diana's grandmother testified against her daughter, Diana's mother, in the custody hearing) contributed to feelings of insecurity, which only intensified as her wedding day approached. At the time of the "wedding of the century," her main interests were children and domesticity. She described herself as "thick as two planks" and, if she did not exactly move sideways, she certainly had the defensive shell.

Fast forward to her late twenties. Talk about a major molt—the world watched one of the remarkable public transformations of the twentieth century. She's probably the most famous person who accomplished a totally different look without cosmetic surgery (rumor had it she dyed her eyelashes, but everything else was bulimia, exercise, and cosmetics). Gone was the mousy brown hair, here comes the bombshell-blonde bob. Gone were the Laura Ashley calf-length pinafores replaced by the tightest and flashiest haute couture. Most people deal with stress by getting angrier, but she only got more gorgeous with each revelation of Walesian marital woes.

Meanwhile, Camilla's own marriage to Andrew Parker Bowles was quietly disintegrating in the countryside. When Camilla and Charles reignited their romance sometime in 1986 (the same year Diana allegedly took up with James Hewitt), the "Di was cast," as it were. The rest, as we know, was a royal soap opera that rolled on for the next decade until the princess's untimely tragic death in a Paris traffic tunnel.

What can we learn from these two wildly divergent personalities both born under the sign of the crab? Both women had a maternal streak (though Camilla seemed to aim hers more at Charles, while Diana focused on Princes William and Harry). Both women had a love of nature, albeit on their own terms. Camilla, an accomplished equestrienne, enjoyed fox hunting and other English countryside pursuits. Diana swam every day, loved the ocean and her tropical beach vacations and according to her former staff, always had rooms filled with fresh flowers.

And where Diana spent the last decade of her life in a constant feint-jab-attack-retreat mode both with her husband and the press, Camilla kept a strict no-comment policy in place—a policy that extended to her family and friends. (Diana, on the other hand, allowed her sisters and girlfriends and staff and others to selectively speak for her). History will be kind to both women, but I suspect that a century from now, Camilla's quiet steadfastness will play better than Diana's Queen of Hearts persona.

Scorpio Friends and Lovers

Magnetic and mesmerizing, loyal and seemingly unshockable, the Scorpio lover is a specialized taste developed by the discriminating. Don't be put off by the image of the scorpion, stinger poised on hoisted tail, claws in *en garde* position. Take under advisement Scorpio's reputation towards being a loner and devil's advocate. Yes, these water signs don't miss a trick and definitely are difficult to fool. But these are qualities that can be excellent in friendship and exciting in a lover.

That Plutonic rulership can sometimes imbue these companions with a taste for the exotic in the boudoir. In their lifetimes, many Scorpios need to try a variety of different sexual activities—even if they secretly are happiest in quilted bathrobes and fuzzy slippers. Shere Hite (November 2), sex researcher, devoted her career to demystifying sexual impulses and putting them in context with current cultural mores. Every generation has a Scorpio lady who basically says, "To hell with the current repressive climate, I'm doing what I please!"

We go from Lady Dorothy Brett (November 10), an artist who had a famous affair with D. H. Lawrence, to Hedy Lamarr (November 9), whose first film appearances in the U.S. were in the nude—and this is in 1933! Lisa Bonet (November 16), tired of her good-girl image on *The Cosby Show*, decided to shake things up with a nude film appearance while still a youth.

As for men, photographer Helmut Newton (October 31) pioneered the use of S&M imagery in fashion photography, a trend that—like it or not—is regularly revived. Actually, the more I think about this, the more one can say that Scorpio often has a very businesslike attitude towards sex. At least in terms of a public image.

But what about regular folks? Here's Donna Lethal, an LA-based Scorpio romantic commenting on what the world expects, and what the reality is: "Scorpios aren't the sex maniacs everyone thinks they are (ever tell someone your sign and watch 'em recoil—or move closer?) and not all of us become messed-up druggies or drunks. Sherlock Holmes must have been a Scorpio. I'm a lot less possessive as I get older. I'm not clingy."*

Scorpio is often attracted to other Scorpios, mainly because there's a built-in, nonverbal understanding. When Scorpios collide, sometimes there's a détente. "Other signs may think we're sneaky, devious, and underhanded but we're just being realistic," they tell themselves. "Just don't get too close."

Scorpio friends will definitely give you some distance and are usually highly unlikely to ask personal questions (Pisces and Cancer can blurt these out but they'd just as soon not. It's the fire and air people who have no problem poking and prying in a personal life). Scorpio friends are also excellent at analyzing situations involving third parties. If something has happened to you on the job or in a relationship, you can learn a lot by sharing the details with a Scorpio.

Pisces Friends and Lovers

Passionate and distracted is the Pisces. They have absolutely *no* problem having crushes for years and sublimating erotic/romantic urges thanks to that dreamy Neptunian rulership. With their innate artistic

---

* Donna Lethal, email message to the author, October 2008.

talent (and occasional proclivity for substance experimentation/abuse) Pisces can be highly latent in their development. Sometimes early sexual experimentation freaks them out so that they're fine living on their own for years, even decades later. That's one extreme.

The other is the Pisces who will write you romantic poetry, pick wildflowers for you, and suggest long walks in the twilight. These are all delightful activities, much appreciated by someone who may be burned out on standard-issue dinner-and-a-movie date etiquette. But as a steady diet, sometimes you may need to say to your Pisces, "Hey, what about doing something with *other* people sometime?"

I've seen Pisces be the life of the party one night and then convinced that people are using them the next. When you're with a Pisces, be prepared for lots of laughs, the occasional tears, and the quirkiest yet astute observations about others. Because they're the last sign of the zodiac, I feel that everything that didn't fit anywhere else gets shoehorned on to their shoulders. Even within their watery element, Pisces puts their own twist on some standard attributes. Thus Scorpio's independence translates into Pisces' ambivalence; Cancer's domesticity is transformed into Piscean nostalgia.

When Pisces folks hear that their symbol is the fish—and that those fish swim in opposite directions—their first reaction is usually a chuckle of recognition. Fish swimming in opposite directions is like one hand clapping, and Pisces can appreciate Zen humor.

Yet where Cancer can come off as self-absorbed and Scorpio may seem cold, Pisces brings a vulnerability to relationships. Your first impression of them is likely to be that they're approachable, accessible, and a little shy. Dig a little deeper and you find Pisces invariably has an interest in arcane matters (my most frequent clients are Gems, followed by fishies). Once their interest is piqued in herbalism, Wicca, numerology, or astrology, they get very deep, very fast. If you've ever been curious about experimenting with a Ouija board, grab a Pisces to share the planchette (heart-shaped indicator). Because Pisces rules the twelfth house governing all that stuff rumbling in our subconsciousness, they have easier access to other psychological realms.

Like Capricorn, Pisces can seem very old and mature before their time, usually in their understanding of human nature. Pisces can be impressively (insanely) tolerant of lovers who are not as sensitive, not as caring as themselves. And when you call them on this, their response is, "I don't have a problem with it."

Of course, if you probe, you'll find they *are* bugged by friends who take advantage. The good friend of a Pisces would be advised to be a listening board, rather than an advisor. The words of one dear Pisces friend still ring in my ear. She and her Virgo girlfriend exemplified a classic "opposites attract" situation. The Virgo brought backbone to the relationship, while the Pisces had a sense of fun. But sometimes backbone and advice isn't what's needed. I remember my Pisces friend remarking after one series of arguments, "I told her I didn't want feedback—I just wanted her to listen!"

Earth signs (and some fire, and some others like Scorpio) always are thinking one step ahead, so the prospect of providing feedback comes naturally. Pisces, on the other hand, wants to explore the experience, turn it over like a rough gemstone and examine all the facets. In a love match with the right partner, Pisces can be a loyal, passionate, and unique partner.

Way back in prehistory, the ancients decided that fire, earth, air, and water summed up the totality of human psychology (and Hippocrates presented these attributes as sanguine, choleric, phlegmatic, and melancholic). Two elements, fire and air are considered masculine and two elements, earth and water, are considered feminine.

Yet why do male water signs sometimes have the most difficult road to travel? As one Scorpio male told me, "I don't know if my own experience is generalizable, but I have always had much easier relationships with, shall we say, 'worthy opponents' among the fixed signs, Taurus, Leo, and Aquarius, than I've ever had with fellow waterworkers. Perhaps because I'm uncomfortable with the risk of them figuring me out before I figure them out."

Water signs are said to be intensely aware of emotions, but society doesn't encourage this degree of introspection for males. I have found that male water signs can be the best-adjusted males in the zodiac—but it's a struggle to get there. Many fall by the wayside in terms of choosing defensiveness over protectiveness, or sulkiness over sensitivity. As they get older and more confident, water sign males can be more comfortable in their skin, especially once they give themselves permission to enjoy their comfort zones.

Of the three elements, Cancer males sometimes have the longest road to travel. Take former president George W. Bush (July 6). Now *there's* an awkwardly adapted Cancer (raised by a pair of Geminis who clearly overlooked the innate sensitivity he had as a child). Yet, he showed his Cancerian colors early on. Take the virtue of loyalty: during the 2000 presidential campaign, he talked about using a number of staff from the Reagan era (even from the Ford era) like Donald Rumsfeld and Dick Cheney. Once elected, he did indeed fill his cabinet with Republican Cold Warriors.

History will show whether the Rumsfeld-led invasion of Iraq was worth the hundreds of billions of our dollars. More egregious was the Bush administration's insensitivity to women's health issues (another Cancer concern) and the environment. Since Cancer rules the stomach, it's not surprising that Dubya's comfort food was straight from his elementary school years: baloney sandwiches. As for Cancer's rulership of the home, he's shown a marked preference for the ranch in Crawford, versus Kennebunkport.

Pisces and Scorpio males generally are wilier about wearing their hearts on their sleeve, so to speak. They can see things clearly but not always act on them directly, whether by choice or disposition. Remember the comments made by Scorpio Neil Young (November 12) about Aquarian Johnny Rotten (January 31) in song: "It's better to burn out than it is to rust." Now remember the album title was *Rust Never Sleeps*, and bear in mind that it's Neil who kept going with an incredibly durable, diffident, forty-some-year career on the comfortable fringes of the music business—it seems to suit him just fine.

Scorpio and Pisces can also be less directed than Cancer. Say they have some compelling insight into someone else's inner workings. Now what? As one Scorpio informant told me, "Culturally, unless there's possible romance brewing, the answer for men is 'nothing,' so it gets ignored or bottled up or stewed-upon or deflected into fantasy. Or, more dangerously, into wit—or drink. Women, on the other hand, are much more tuned in emotionally. And they have the option of girl talk, gossip, intrigue, and scheming. Are these necessarily any healthier? At least they have a range of conventional outlets."

Pisces tends toward understanding the view from other people's shoes. (Scorpio understands why they want those shoes!) And Pisces can wear a mask as readily as they can present themselves. Male Pisces actors, writers, and performers can be absorbed into a persona in a way the other two water signs won't. Tom Wolfe (March 2) has a flashiness, but his journalism is as probing as any in the twentieth century. Roger Daltrey (March 1) took on Pete Townshend's personality and passions when he sang his bandmate's songs.

Now, Scorpio men can have a mania that extends to an obsessiveness about seeing how things work, or seeing what makes things tick (part of Scorpio's thematic inheritance is surgery—and there's no better way to get inside a situation!). Consider Sam Donaldson (March 11), Pisces news-star who was distinctive about his news style, but wasn't a hardcore news analyst. Contrast his style with Scorpios Walter Cronkite (November 4) and Dan Rather (October 31). Those two wrestled with the news on a moral level (not always to their benefit, although more so for Uncle Walter than for Rather).

Finally, we come to the elephant in the room: alcoholism and substance abuse. Water signs more than any other element are connected with alcoholism, addiction, and drug abuse and are the classic tortured artist, hell-bent on self-destruction. Which brings us to ...

Water Sign Preoccupations, Obsessions, and Addictions

For water signs, these really run the gamut: food, drink, emotionally satisfying relationships, artistic pursuits, people who behave predictably, nature, outdoors, the ocean, living by water, sailing and swimming, cooking, children, gardening (a trait they share with earth signs), and relaxing. Water sign folks like their creature comforts and are very fond of comfy chairs and couches, pillows, and places to unwind. They can also be enthusiastic foodies who seek out unusual recipes, or contrive their own sauces, dishes, and creations.

If you are the object of obsession for someone born under a water sign or who has enormous water sign influence, you're in for some intense courtship, particularly if you're being pursued by a Cancer or Scorpio. Pisces can have passionate feelings for someone but they need to be very secure to share this with the object of their affection. If you are interested in one of these signs, bear in mind that all water signs love analyzing others' motives and are highly sensitive to insincerity. Also, water signs (like earth signs) tend to have strong mating instincts. Casual interaction isn't usually for them.

Water sign folks can be amazingly nonmaterialistic, and even though they understand the value of an oriental rug versus an off-the-rack eight-by-ten shag, they can live with either. Like earth signs, they can be possessive about their collections, but they can also show a surprising streak of generosity. Their philosophy—whether they know it or not—is to go with the flow, and they'd just as soon avoid direct confrontation.

It should be noted that Western industrialized society can be very cruel and insensitive to the male water sign nature. That impulse to nurture doesn't generally go over well in the armed forces, locker room, or other typically masculine domains. Sometimes male water signs need a lifetime to come to the terms with the fact that they get tearful at sentimental movies or music. So they end up protecting themselves with a veneer of sarcasm or insouciance. The wise friend or lover of a water sign will understand that such an affect is only skin-deep. Or is that *fin-* and *shell-*deep?

Water Sign Work and Careers: Choosing a Career That Will Fuel Your Soul

Water signs can choose a career path at an early age, expressed as a generalized desire: for example, "helping people," "teaching children," "protecting the environment," or "working with plants." Water sign folks can bring an inimitable sensitivity to others and an uncanny ability to anticipate others' moods. Their biggest challenge is finding a career that fulfills their need to connect with others emotionally and intellectually (up to a point), and also allows them room to grow. I would advise parents of water sign kids to give them structure and encouragement to experiment. Don't hem them in early or urge them to do just one thing. When they're in college, they absolutely should experiment with a range of courses and even majors. Remember the adage: water seeks its own level. Water signs like working with others who share their point of view and are sometimes more drawn to a group of people rather than a particular field.

Generally, water signs aren't in it for the money, although they certainly are capable of working hard and earning well. They can also spend pretty freely and have unrealistic ideas about exactly how much they need in terms of funding. All three water signs are happy and fulfilled if they work with those who need lots of help, and most of my water sign clients have a career in which nurturing others plays a big role. Vague feelings of water sign guilt over having so much can be assuaged by improving the world, one person at a time.

Cancer Careers, Coworkers, and Bosses

The Moon rules the home and hearth as well as our fourth zodiac sign. That lunatic influence can produce some very interesting careers. The Moon rules baking and any profession to do with the water and tides. Cancer is the crab, so a job involving a protective carapace or a costume that needs to be periodically shed (molted) could be an aspect of a profession.

Cancer is security-minded, so jobs involving personal or financial security or protected places could be a good fit. For fun, let's take a look at that baking influence. Since the sign rules that profession, a comfortable Cancerian occupation could involve manipulating things with their hands. I remember years back getting a new Cancer client who wanted to make a change from her office job. Instantly, the image of a woman baking flew into my head, but instead I said, "Have you considered taking a ceramics class?" She had, and it was something she was excited about doing again.

Working with clay, or even learning about massage, can be a Cancerian pursuit. The hospitality business is also a place where one can find Cancers, although there is a burnout factor here since the sign can take others' dissatisfactions to heart. Cancer can make good therapists, or help others recovering from an event or making a big decision, so guidance counseling or working in a rehab could be satisfying. Working with plants, either in a greenhouse or as a florist or in some other capacity is a Cancer interest. I have a brilliant and cuspy Cancer cousin who was in the first wave of computer science majors. He has developed a unique career bridging botany and academia by doing high-level analysis of rainforest plants.

Locations where Cancer can be happy include kitchens or places where making things happens; also environments with babies in them, or locations near the water. If asked, always recommend a Cancer kid take an oceanography class in college!

Cancer should be aware that their own nature is to wax and wane,
so a topic that interests them passionately can also be something they
outgrow or lose interest in over time. Cancer also needs to be careful
about whom they're working with. The fact that they carry their stress
in their stomach means that difficult bosses can affect them more than,
say, a Scorpio (who's got a natural self-protectiveness) or a Pisces (who
can zone out at will).

I remember reading the following sentence in someone's blog once:
"I can't believe my coworker got fired—this is terrible, just awful! I
mean, who am I going to have lunch with?" The writer was—sorry, but
not surprising to say—a Cancer. And this is a great example of Cancer
at their most self-absorbed and self-serving.

Fortunately, more crabs do not take this particular tack when it
comes to their comfort in careers. Cancer coworkers can seem stand-
offish at first but invariably—like 99.44 percent of the time—that behavior is strictly a byproduct of crustacean shyness. A Cancer coworker will notice if you have the sniffles or if you seem peaky. They'll offer
tissues, aspirin, and a cup of hot tea, and then make one for themselves

to keep you company. Cancerian coworkers are complete mysteries to some people and utterly beloved by others.

Cancer needs to be very careful about how that reputation for loyalty is used. At most jobs (judging from what I've heard from many crabbies), their loyalty is underappreciated. If things are going wrong at a job, they're more likely to stick it out and be miserable rather than jump ship. Cancer is a very patient sign and although you may think they're not happy in a position (because of what they're saying) chances are, they've adapted to circumstances and are just venting.

Cancer bosses can be incredibly thoughtful and insightful with people who work for them. They also have a wide range of motion and can get along with very different people. Discreet and highly sensitive to social currents, Cancer bosses at their best can surpass expectations. Those who are going through a difficult time or who are at a turning point in the career (but are still the boss) can seem flaky or unexpectedly emotional. Cancer does *not* like conflict or confrontation, so if you find they are inconsistent about their mandates, approach with caution.

Scorpio Careers, Coworkers, and Bosses

I've had some excellent Scorpio editors in my years as a journalist (ditto Cancer), and I've seen this sign take an amazing array of jobs. Its themes of the eighth house—sex, death, and other people's money— can cover a wide array of professions, from therapy to mortuary science or religious pursuits, to banking and estate law. In fact, I once knew a Gemini woman who was passionate about her job as a paralegal in a law firm specializing in estate planning. She didn't strike one as a typical twin as she was quiet and modest and not divided in her personality. When I took a closer look at her chart, I noticed Scorpio aspects everywhere. So the Scorpionic influence made her very precise and perfectionistic when it came to the paperwork of probate and the Gemini influence helped her be a clear communicator.

Until the 1930s, Scorpio was traditionally ruled by Mars, but with the discovery of Pluto, Scorpio got a new ruler. Pluto is, of course, the god of the underworld, and as the gods go, Pluto is a take-no-prisoners kind of influence. If there are problems that come to light, that's Pluto. If there's a higher justice that needs to be served—beyond Mercurial even-stevens, even beyond Jupiter's judgments—Pluto will sort things out. Resurrection is an interest and the transition from life to death to whatever's next can fascinate Scorps.

What kind of career will make mysterious and intense Scorpios happy? One in which there is autonomy, but also a chance to work predominantly with people whose expertise is respected. One of my favorite favorite references, the *A to Z Horoscope Maker and Delineator*, first published at the turn of the last century, cites just two occupations as appropriate to those with Plutonic influence: gunner and psychoanalyst.

So, let me get this straight, you might say: the best careers for Scorps are those in which they destroy others or dissect them psychologically? Ouch! Seriously, though, let's look at locations in which Scorpio would be comfortable. Pluto ruling the underworld doesn't necessarily rule out a fresh-air-and-sunshine environment for Scorpio; I've known plenty who are crazy about plants . . . grown under a UV bulb. Scorpio can enjoy work that involves research, particularly of people who have passed on, so a variety of academic pursuits would make them happy. Scorpio is very happy working in a bar or tavern or place where escapism is the order of the day. I've seen Scorpio be very satisfied in nursing homes or caring for Alzheimer's patients. Scorpio also rules surgery, so working with knives (actual surgery, butchery, culinary arts, woodworking) would be a natural. So is working with the disenfranchised (a water sign theme).

Scorpio's wide range of motion also puts them in line for surprising and super-suitable jobs that few other signs would take on, starting with saint (note, these are the days these saints are celebrated, not necessarily their birthdays). My favorite is St. Martin de Porres (November 3). A very interesting saint, he was the out-of-wedlock son of a Spanish nobleman and a freed African slave, and grew up in poverty in Peru. He later apprenticed with a surgeon-barber (very Scorpionic), learned medicine, and learned how to care for the sick. He was skilled at urging the wealthy to contribute to his Dominican priory and eventually founded an orphanage, children's hospital, and even a shelter for stray cats and dogs. Elizabeth, mother of St. John the Baptist (November 5), had a late pregnancy and was visited by Mary soon after the Annunciation. Pope Leo the Great (November 10) protected Rome from Attilla the Hun. And, of course, All Saints' Day and All Souls' Day come on November 1 and 2.

Sex worker/promoter is another interesting Scorpio job. Take Larry Flynt (November 1), Shere Hite (November 2), or *Playboy* First Daughter and publisher Christie Hefner (November 8). Along the same lines you'll find the role of sexpot. How about Hedy Lamarr (November 9) or Vivien Leigh (November 5)? Then there's the sidekick: Peter Cook (November 17) and Dick Smothers (November 21).

Here's a stretch—Scorpio rules surgery. Have you ever thought about how skates are like knives? Some graceful ice champions include

Sasha Cohen (October 26), Paul Wylie (October 28), Evgeni Plushenko (November 3), Tonya Harding (November 12), Xue Shen (November 13), Oksana Baiul (November 16), Alexei Urmanov (November 17), and Jenni Meno (November 19). Tomboy-style child star is another Scorpio job. Consider Tatum O'Neal (November 5) and Jodie Foster (November 19). Scorpio can also be a masterful strategist—just ask Hillary Clinton (October 26). These people have plenty of fashion sense, too. Excellent style arbiters include the alleged inspiration for *The Devil Wears Prada*, *Vogue* editor Anna Wintour (November 3) and editor Tina Brown (*Vanity Fair*, *New Yorker*, *Talk* magazine) (November 21). Finally, Scorpio rules *actual* surgery: Christiaan Barnard (November 8).

Pisces Careers, Coworkers, and Bosses

The last sign of the zodiac is remarkably flexible and usually comes with many natural talents. Neptune is the planetary ruler and the twelfth house, which offers influence, rules the subconscious, hidden attributes, and secrets. All very dramatic and very exciting for someone like me to analyze, without a doubt. Locations for Pisces include photography studios (including x-ray/radiology departments), backstage at a theater or other public place (i.e., the nonpublic locations), places where cleaning happens, places where visionary experiences occur, or transformative experiences.

Neptune is all about mystical, mediumistic experiences and I've never known a Pisces who wasn't crazy about listening to music. I've known many Pisces who are amazing musicians, folks who can pick up anything from accordion to zither and be instantly fluent. That ease can also set up expectations for Pisces that make following a set path or maintaining consistent discipline in a field very difficult. Whereas some signs (earth element folks, some fire folks, the fixed signs) welcome a roadmap, Pisces would just as soon break ground in their own way.

But this is an adaptable sign and Pisces is usually excellent at fitting into any kind of work environment. Before long, they're the folks who seem to know how everything works: from how to set the alarm, to the right place to hit the copy machine to get the paper path clear again. Pisces jobs can include administrative jobs in the arts and performance world, teaching special education (and working with those who are psychologically challenged), and nursing, especially clinician work. Pisces is fairly unshockable but also has an appetite to be outrageous, so work that involves a mask or makeup or some kind of disguise would amuse them. Or creating these kinds of disguises. Working with waste or recyclable materials is also a Piscean theme.

Pisces I've known who have a job in the straight world (i.e., the world of business or government or manufacturing) somehow carve out their own niche. They can figure out how to use fractions of pennies or tiny units of database to create a market. Remember, the image of Pisces is fish swimming in different directions, a seeming paradox. Pisces coworkers can be hilarious—able to see the humor or short-sightedness in corporate environments. They usually know what fire escape to hang out on for a smoke break and they're amused by she-nanigans that can happen in office culture. If you work with a Pisces, you may think they're goofing off, but somehow, they'll get work completed. Pisces can be masterful procrastinators, and sometimes rely on that shot of adrenaline to get things done. "Just don't ask me to present at the meeting" is a classic Pisces comment, but if push comes to shove and they have to speak, they'll be eloquent, humorous, and informative and seem to connect with everyone in the room.

If you work with a Pisces, they will be highly appreciative of any eccentric behavior. Chances are, there's a gadget from a curio shop somewhere on their desk. Perhaps they have a collection of quirky Asian soda cans, or bobbing-head dogs. For all their waifish affect, Pisces have a very sarcastic side and chances are, if you're venting, they'll have even more to share. Tardiness can be a Pisces attribute, but they're usually fine staying late. With Pisces, they'd just as soon continue what they've been doing.

Pisces bosses really have to grow into the job, and this can take years. I've known Pisces who've organized musical groups and who consistently pull an "I'm not in charge" commentary while loading equipment and signing an inventory sheet. Pisces is scrupulous—if they do end up running the show, they're highly sensitive to others whose work habits may be questionable, or who are less reliable than needed. Pisces bosses are very comfortable filling in the blanks for others.

five

ASTROLOGICAL MATCHUPS, THE SAME ELEMENTS

In the Laboratory—Mixing and Matching the Elements

Okay, you've read about the four elements, and should have a grasp on some key principles. Now, put on your white smock and let's venture into the astrological elemental compatibility laboratory. What happens when you mix elements together? Does fire plus fire equal twice as much fire? Or does the calculus add up to an exponential impact? Can two fire signs working together get four times as much work done? And do two water signs combining make for more sensitivity or less?

We'll start with some simple combos: fire plus fire, earth plus earth, air plus air, and water plus water. You can learn a lot by close observation of your own reactions to those of different elemental families. I always emphasize this part of astrology to clients when we have our first meeting. I ask them to answer some questions about friends and lovers including, "Are there signs (ergo, elements) that you are consistently drawn to? Or signs that make you absolutely crazy? Perhaps there are signs that used to be in your life quite often but in recent years have become less appealing."

This book is arranged in sections, so that every possible combination of sign plus sign is represented. That's eighty-four combinations in all. We'll start by combining the same element in this chapter. I have also included astrological neighbors—the signs that are next door to one another, for example Aries, the first sign, plus Taurus, the second sign. And I conclude with astrological opposites, the signs that are 180 degrees apart. Which, in the capricious way of astrology, can often amount to that "opposites attract" dynamic.

Fire Plus Fire

So much in common—so many areas for conflict. Fire signs together can keep each other young, excited, and on their toes. They can also make for a scorched-earth policy in the immediate vicinity. Remember the 2000 campaign and how absent Leo President Bill Clinton was from Aries Al Gore's rhetoric and appearances? Would Gore have carried some swing states had Clinton been more visible? Instead, Gore did a maverick Aries maneuver and figured he could go it alone. But then he hooked up with then-Democrat Joe Lieberman—an Aquarian, thus not easily led. Yes, we knew these guys were faithful to their wives, as was opponent George W. Bush, but the Democratic ticket didn't galvanize the electorate. Better for Gore to have ridden on a few inches of Clinton's coattails. Fire and fire can learn a lot from each other as well as inspire the other to burn ever so much brighter.

Aries and Aries

Whoa, who thinks *this* is a good idea? People looking for unique charismatic compatibility who have a high tolerance for egocentricity. *Star Trek* producer Gene Roddenberry created the most enduring science fiction partnership ever when he cast Leonard Nimoy (March 26) as the unflappable Mr. Spock opposite the volatile Canadian actor William Shatner (March 22). Granted, Shatner is just zero degrees of Aries, but still. Add fire to fire and you get conflagration; even though *Star Trek* is probably the most famous example of how to make a fortune in syndication and licensing, these two men spent many of their adult years post-*Trek* making snide comments about one another. Still, they managed to crank out a festival's worth of *Star Trek* films, thus encouraging subsequent generations "to boldly go where no man has gone before." Now, if only these guys could get past their beef with Mr. Sulu/George Takei (April 20, if you're curious).

Aries and Leo

This is a fabulous pairing—and super for professional connections. Aries can be the baby in this relationship, which can bring out Leo's protective, mentor tendencies. Romantic poet/rock star/bondage poet-peer Algernon Swinburne (April 5) found great support from older poet Alfred, Lord Tennyson (August 6), who managed to overlook his peccadilloes and swinish behavior in favor of praising his poetry, which had moments of genius.

In the twentieth century, outgoing author Kingsley Amis (April 16) had a longtime friendship with recessive poet Philip Larkin (August 9). They were always able to overlook temperamental differences and forged a strong and intellectually satisfying friendship. Amis was effusive and constantly in pursuit of fame and success, while Larkin was neurotic and shy, and though well known as a poet, spent the majority of his days as a librarian. (Some might say the friendship endured because they spent so little time in one another's company.)

Professional success was the product of the work relationship between filmmaker Blake Edwards (July 26) and composer Henry Mancini (April 16). The opening notes of the *Pink Panther* theme will forever emblemize their witty, sly, humorous take. And designer Oleg

Cassini (April 11) had a famously successful partnering with then-First Lady Jackie Kennedy (July 28). The ram made the lioness look like a queen by making her wardrobe more simple but elegant. Aries are often brilliant at cutting to the chase and Cassini's touch with streamlined A-line silhouettes was peerless.

An Aries and Leo partnership will also work if both sides have the same attitude about what kind of recognition is required. John Stockton (March 26) was brilliant at strategizing basketball moves. He found an ideal partner in Karl Malone (July 24). Both of them were able to anticipate what needed to happen next on the court. And neither was a greedhog for attention in a sport that encourages showboating on a grand scale. Then again, Al Gore was an Aries married to a Leo—who shared a birthday with his boss, Bill Clinton. Harmony goes only so far!

Aries and Sagittarius

Aries will usually take the lead, and rams seem even more straightforward when compared to archers. Look no further than David Letterman (April 12) and Paul Shaffer (November 27). Don't believe me? Try Alec Baldwin (April 3) and Kim Basinger (December 8). The Baldwin/Basinger marriage had some highly public fall-out, culminating with Baldwin's book about how divorced dads always get the short end of the stick. (Note: I've been in the same room as Mr. Baldwin, back when he and Basinger were making *The Marrying Man*. He was very dissatisfied with the production company, and this was a tabloid story in the early nineties. He had no problem taking the lead on his complaints no matter what the setting; I can vouch that he's got oodles of personal charisma.) Sagittarius and Aries should be able to laugh together, and in a successful pairing, Sadge can appreciate Aries' energy, while Aries values Sagittarian wisdom—or, more likely, amusing eccentricies.

Leo and Leo

Like their namesake lion, Leos prefer to travel in a pride. When I work with Leo clients and ask them to list their good friends' birthdays, invariably, Leos will cite a few other lions. Yet do they make good love partners for one another? Absolutely, but it's a passionate pairing. There will always be some jockeying for position that might play out in public. Both signs are literal-minded, and both signs need a lot of personal attention. So how does this work? With assistants and lots of bustle. Leos can respect one another but generally are happiest if they are the top lion in the pack.

Leo and Sagittarius

"Enabling" has become a dirty word in recent times, but when you think about Leo and Sagittarius together, it's unusual that the Leo *isn't* the leader, helpmate, or crutch when needed. Leo's pride (vanity?) is utterly at odds with Sagittarius' pell-mell, impulsive, accident-prone way of being. Leo is capable of being childish with the world, but when they have a Sagittarius to take care of, out come the bandages and soothing words of reassurance. If you're the Leo in this relationship, prepare yourself for the occasional Sadge tantrum or episode of running away (from responsibility, obligations made, etc.).

With a lot of patience and a willingness to overlook the occasional outburst, this can be an enduring relationship. If you're the Sagittarius in this relationship, figure that Leo *will* try to boss you around and will *not* rest until you are doing what they think you *should be* doing. You can survive this by reminding yourself of the following: they have your best interests at heart and want to keep you going. It will always be vexing for the Sagittarius to repeatedly hear things like, "Tie your shoes!" "Can you drive within the speed limit?" "Do you see that cliff up ahead?" But you have to ask yourself: is it worth getting angry and defying them, or will it take a really, really long time to recover from this cliff fall?

Here is a fabulous lion and archer matchup: Mick Jagger (July 26) and Keith Richards (December 18). Keith wouldn't still be here if it wasn't for Mick Jagger's willingness to keep him alive (well, Mick plus various wives and girlfriends, as well as dedicated medical teams . . .). Keith is the most famous bad boy in rock'n' roll. He makes the cat with nine lives look like a shirker. These two have been friends since childhood and though "Keef" may have groused about Mick's show-biz musical tastes (compared to his own more authentic Chicago/Memphis/Mississippi guitar influences), the Glimmer Twins shine more brightly as a unit.

Another can be found in the aristocracy: Queen Elizabeth, (the Queen Mother, August 5), and King George VI (December 14). George had a stammer that was so pronounced there were grave doubts of his ability to serve as king. Queen Elizabeth got him a top-rate speech therapist to assist him practicing speeches and, more importantly, shared her boundless Leo confidence with her reluctant mate. These two were *the* royal double-act in the twentieth century.

Sagittarius and Sagittarius

Independent and anarchic, Sagittarius doesn't really need others in the way that baby-faced Aries and childlike Leo do. Sagittarius isn't dependent on praise or approval and they will follow their own whims more than other fire signs. Wanderers by nature, when a Sadge comes across another Sadge there can be an incandescent partnership that excludes all others. Because the centaur is, like Pisces' fish and Gemini's twins, essentially two-in-one (one part a beast!), Sagittarius can spend many years amusing others yet being misunderstood by the general public. However, the humor Sagittarians create together can be enormously amusing—and intimidating to a third party.

For the most part, these signs together are all about creating a force of good. Birthday buddies Dick Van Dyke (December 13) and Morey Amsterdam (December 14) had a good-natured chemistry on Van Dyke's eponymous breakout TV sitcom, a show that has stood the test of time. The scenes in the writers' room, where Van Dyke interacted with Amsterdam's character Buddy, are models of good gag-writing in which jokes build upon jokes.

You'd think these two-of-a-kind pairings might cancel each other out, but here's a fabulous literary union: Louisa May Alcott and her feckless but brilliant educator father, Bronson Alcott. They even share a birthday: November 29. Bronson was one of the founding Transcendentalists in Concord, but along the way had numerous failed business and lecturing ventures though he famously founded the first integrated school in America. He brought the family to Fruitlands for a winter of living communally with like-minded souls (an adventure Louisa caricatured in *Transcendental Wild Oats*), where all subsisted only on wizened apples and cold water and froze in flax clothing (cotton exploited slaves, wool exploited sheep). Louisa adored her father and, had he been a success, she might never have felt the economic need to provide a living for the family with her *own* pen. And so we basically have Bronson (and Ticknor and Fields, her publisher) to thank for *Little Women*.

Earth Plus Earth

Who takes the initiative in this relationship? It depends on other factors in the horoscope, but usually Taurus will trump the other signs when it comes to what-and-where queries. The advantages that occur when two earth signs find one another are consistency, and usually a certain level of financial stability. With some very rare exceptions in the many clients I've had through the years, those with earth sign Suns or dominant earth sign influence in their chart seldom have money troubles.

When earth signs bond with one another romantically, there can be tremendous strength and endurance, but there's also inertia. In a workplace, a group of earth signs collaborating on accounting, database management, financial concerns, and budget can be highly effective.

Taurus and Taurus

Okay, in some cities in Spain and Mexico they see this all the time in the bull ring, and wouldn't you know it? The bulls never have a problem with each other. So it is with *Homo sapiens*, albeit with healthy respect, distance, and deference. I had a unique insight into this particular combination years ago, while watching a TV show devoted to the career of Barbra Streisand. There were lots of film clips and celebrity celebrators, but among the latter, Shirley MacLaine, who shares Barbra's April 24 birthday, had the most penetrating insights to share.

MacLaine (born seven years before Streisand, in 1934) noted the many Taurean tendencies they share: "She's very attracted to sensual specifics, notices perfume, and will know the name. She'll notice if someone has had a tooth capped. . . . Gets depressed when others don't live up to their brilliance." The presumption, of course, is that Streisand, and, by inference, MacLaine *always* live up to their brilliance. (This is demonstrable for both: the number of performers with Emmy and Grammy and Oscar *and* Tony awards on their mantelpieces is slender indeed. You want tenacity? Hire a Taurus.) Yet these two women have never worked together, a fact that perhaps contributes to ongoing amity. Though wouldn't they be fabulous in a remake of *Hush . . . Hush, Sweet Charlotte?*

Taurus and Virgo

Again, mutual respect can definitely prevail, but Virgo's habit of nitpicking and Taurus' habit of drawing a line in the sand and refusing to budge can make for difficulties in relationships. If both signs understand that they are seeing each other *as parodies* of themselves, they can function well together. If they are coworkers, there should be a third person both can report to. Most astrology books will tell you that two-of-a-kind, in terms of elements, can have a lot in common, but in the field, I've seen more disparities. What can happen with these two earth signs is that they go to extremes: Taurus will become extremely stubborn; Virgo will get defensive and then critical. Without an arbiter, this can go nowhere. However, if there is a battle to be fought, or an argument to be made, Taurus and Virgo can line up together very quickly.

Taurus and Capricorn

Capricorn really should be the dominant player in this relationship, if only because they're willing to out-stubborn the Taurus. If these two signs are in a work relationship with one another, and they have extremely tangential interactions, this can be a fine combination. If they are in business together, chances are the Taurus will be the one worrying about the outreach, where Capricorn will busy themselves with inventory. But, as we've seen, Capricorn really does function perfectly well on their own, and Taurus is also content with autonomy (albeit enjoying their role in a group—or herd). In a romantic relationship, one or both folks should be at the beginning or end of the sign if there's going to be some dynamic interaction. I've seen romances between these two signs that literally fall apart from sheer boredom and monotony. Both signs can get stuck in the mud, either behaviorally or emotionally, and then it will take a third party (a child? another lover?) to get things rolling again.

Virgo and Virgo

"I feel the earth/Move/Under my feet." Um, no, actually. Two Virgos together can have a great friendship with lots of mutual support until one of them makes a suggestion that makes the other uncomfortable.

Since Virgo is the mutable earth sign, these two can understand one another's neuroses more effectively than others. If I had a health question, or was trying to figure out how to put an Ikea bookshelf together, I would definitely want these two signs helping, despite their strong ability to drive one another crazy. This relationship can seem mystifying to those on the outside. With both being so picky, so quick to see flaws, two Virgos can fuel each other's outrage. By the time onlookers think these two are ready to explode, one or both Virgos erupt into laughter. Nothing like keeping everyone else on their toes!

Virgo and Capricorn

If these were playing cards, we're talking the difference between the jack of hearts and the ace of spades. Capricorn tends to be very single-minded, as does Virgo. At their best, these two earth elements can combine into a material stronger than steel, but something happens when these two signs collide, and usually it's Virgo taking a backseat. Capricorn sometimes erroneously has a reputation for being taciturn, but I've known plenty of chatty goats, whose level of recall for the most mundane details is phenomenal. Again, these are two signs you want to see working together in a financial situation or on a construction site. They can cooperate on projects, but both will think the other is *such* a perfectionist!

Capricorn and Capricorn

Heavy for others, yet highly satisfactory for the Capricorns. Finally— someone who thinks Just Like Me. Someone who wants to take their time and consider all the worst-case options. Someone who enjoys material comfort and also has an eye for value. Caps together are formidable for other people, and you do not want to get in their way. This is also a highly solvent pairing, able to make longterm plans and work towards a goal that seems enormous in its scope. For a sign with truly solitary, self-enclosed tendencies, another Cap can be reassuring and bring out some essential aspects of the personality.

The example I found that shows an interesting working relationship is Mary Tyler Moore (December 29) and Betty White (January 17). If you've seen episodes of the classic seventies sitcom *The Mary Tyler Moore Show*, you may remember Mary never seemed quite so innocent and naïve as when she was onscreen with White's predatory character, the "Happy Homemaker" Sue Ann Nivens. And White's character took special relish in her willingness to shock.

Air Plus Air

This combination is great fun, but can definitely leave people breathless, exhausted, and confused. If one of the players is an Aquarius male, there can be real confusion about who said they'd do what. Or what exactly was decided. Air signs are masters at keeping things vague and in play—just because they're good at juggling, others can easily be dazzled. When two air signs collide romantically, one of them always ends up relying upon more stable elements in their own astrological chart.

For example: Put two air signs together. One has a fire sign Moon (volatile emotions), and the other has an earth sign Moon (stable, but stubborn emotions). The air sign with the earth sign Moon will always seem more like an earth sign than an air sign when confronted with someone who has heavy helpings of air and fire, purely out of defense.

Gemini and Gemini

My boilerplate comments to (and about) Gemini is that they are the one sign in the zodiac who really *does* fit with everyone, mostly because the vagaries of their splintered personalities can find an easy fit. And though you may not agree with their politics, or the dynasty they have inflicted upon America in the late twentieth century, you have to admire George and Barbara Bush for the endurance of their own partnership.

Two Gems together (she's June 8, he's June 12) and you might first think: who's in charge here?

What undoubtedly made the choices easier for the Bushes, who have been married since World War II, is the fact that they came of age in an era when gender roles were much more clearly defined. Both come from mainline WASP families with inherited money, and both had political antecedents: Barbara Pierce is connected to nineteenth-century president Franklin Pierce; George is a senator's son.

At the outset, they both seem like cookie-cutter examples of privilege and connections. But their lives got very interesting once George decided to go into the oil business and moved the family to Texas. Yes, they sent their kids to privileged Eastern schools, and continued summering at the compound in Kennebunkport. But the fact that in the 1950s, both were up for a very outside-the-box adventure for people of their class is notable, and a tribute to Gemini's curiosity and willingness to try something new.

The partnership aspects of Gemini Sun are also a strong motif. Bush senior's business and later political career was assisted by a network of cronies and senior advisors every step of the way. Gemini is excellent at making friends and can also use social abilities to his or her own merit.

Gemini and Libra

See "Gemini and Pisces" for another variant on funny business teams, but I've also noted that Gemini and Libra can be a dynamic combination for performance and writing. One partnership that has literally shaped worldwide generations of children is Muppet impresario/inventor Jim Henson (September 24) and performer Frank Oz (May 24). Air signs can take inspiration easily and the cosmology of the Muppet world has influenced several generations in basic skills (number and letter recognition, songs and stories). These two air signs can feed off each other's creativity and be tremendously productive. The challenge is paring down myriad influences. Deadlines will help in this relationship as far as business is concerned. As for love—these two can have a marvelous time together, but at some point, a grown-up may need to step in so something gets finished.

Gemini and Aquarius

What happens when a self-sufficient air sign meets the air sign with two personalities? Who floats into the sky faster? When these two signs collide, it can be electric; if Gemini has any plans to reign in Aquarius, they're usually disappointed. Both of these signs need stability for their best qualities to shine. A distraction level can set in as well. Oddly enough, this is a combination that can bring out the stable, consistent, pattern-seeking side of Aquarius. While Gemini can be completely unruly and ungovernable, Aquarius can be at their most efficient and helpful. The plus side of this pairing is that the socially responsible aspects of both signs can flourish. Air signs can be unintentionally solipsistic—a by-product of living in their heads; a reminder that there's a wider world can be a boon.

Libra and Libra

A battle of wills can erupt when air with leadership meets similar unless responsibilities are clearly defined, or one Libra decides to play a caretaking role. Two Libras together can definitely be very twinlike—anticipating one another's thoughts and ideas and finishing sentences. Two Libras can be in business together, and they can be personally involved. And if the universe is kind, they'll be surrounded by many water and earth sign folks to provide some much needed stability. But Libra can amuse each other in a way that no other sign possibly could. Carrie Fisher (October 21) was briefly married to singer/songwriter Paul Simon (October 13). Both are highly verbal and high-strung so it was an interesting relationship, but didn't have a lot of staying power.

Simon's next wife was the very different, quirkily sultry Pisces chanteuse Edie Brickell (March 10).

Groucho Marx (October 2) and Margaret Dumont (October 20) had an irresistible relationship on film. They appeared in seven movies together, and Dumont, whose career hitherto had been that of a dignified dowager, was soon completely undone by the caperings, jibes, and ad-libs of her grease-mustachioed costar. Harpo, Chico, and Groucho presented an impenetrable trinity of comedy for years in the twentieth century; Dumont was the only outside player whose presence was essential to their comedy.

Libra and Aquarius

Lots of fun when these two combine, though not a lot of consistency. Making plans and keeping them is probably the purview of the Libra, although an Aquarius born really close to Pisces will feel more responsible about follow-through. These two air signs can be highly compatible as long as things never get too heavy or serious. Carole Lombard (October 6) and Clark Gable (February 1) were as hot a romance as one can imagine in the 1930s. Lombard, the brilliant blonde screwball comedienne, and Gable, smoldering and constantly bemused, stood for glamour and a certain lightness that was most welcome in Depression-era America.

Aquarius and Aquarius

People of the same sign tend to understand one another even if they don't always agree or relate. If one Aquarian is in a subordinate position (i.e., employee or child), the person in charge is likely to feel more responsible for guiding the other water carrier along. Aquarius is so independent that the presence of another independent Aquarius could cause some anxiety. However, if I had a publishing house and needed someone to think of plot lines for fantasy books, I'd want a troupe of

Aquarians on the payroll. Ironically, an Aquarian will be most annoyed by Aquarian traits (flightiness, lack of ability to commit) they see in their partner. There's a great learning experience to be had by both signs should they meet and mate.

Water Plus Water

The intermingled emotionality of two or more water signs together can be intimidating to those less in touch with their feelings than these insightful folks. If there's one thing to watch out for when water collides with water, it's a flood of feelings. Generally, when times are tough for one, they're not so bad for the other, so there can be turn-taking that gets everyone through the difficult times. As for positive aspects of water plus water, think of the insight, the caring, the thoughtfulness, the artistic sensitivity, and the nurturing that can ensue. Bear in mind, however, that you folks have less in common with one another than the other three elements, and your potential to drive each other bonkers is very high.

Yes, I've known instances of happy partnerships among the water signs—particularly business partnerships—but for the most part, each water sign has such a blueprint of self-identity leaving little room for others. A Cancer will cancel out another Cancer, and a Cancer can be hurt by Scorpio's sting (while Scorpio can dismiss Cancers who aren't super-nurturing as whiners). A Scorpio can be amused by Pisces, and Scorps usually get along wonderfully with other Scorpios—as long as everyone keeps a respectful distance. Pisces with other Pisces can turn into couch potatoes faster than you can say "EZ chair with ottoman." If the TV remote control gets lost, these two can have a happy argument deciding who's turn it is to get it next.

Cancer and Cancer

Directed and determined, protective and feisty: when Cancers collide there can be what I think of as "instamacy," the immediate recognition of a like-minded soul. But can this last? The jury's still out as far as I'm concerned—and please feel free to write me if you beg to differ. Cancer likes other folks who are sensitive but pretty much figures no one else will have their depth of caring and insight. If you are in a committed relationship with a Cancer that has proved the test of time, I would bet that a big factor in your success is that both of you are capable of instant sympathy without guidance. Sometimes Cancer just likes to vent, and if they're questing for an answer, it's subordinate to their need to process out loud.

Cancer and Scorpio

I've known Scorpios who claim that Cancer *always* drives them crazy and Cancers who say they've *never* met a Scorpio they trusted except for those born at the beginning of the sign when there's a peace-seeking Libra influence, or at the end where the imminent Sagittarius Sun lightens the load. Nevertheless, to give you an idea of this sign's improbable romantic range of motion, consider this: Both Princess Diana and Camilla Parker Bowles were born under the sign of Cancer; Prince Charles is a true-blue Scorpio. (See the chapter on water signs for more on Diana, Charles, and assorted cast members in the royal soap opera.)

Still, this relationship has its own kind of crazy logic, but it takes a lot of patience on both sides. Both Cancer and Scorpio can be irrationally stubborn; both animals come equipped with claws! There can also be unconventional relationships between the two, such as that of Elsa Lanchester (October 28) and Charles Laughton (July 1). Elsa was a brilliant and eccentric stage actor, most famous for portraying the Bride of Frankenstein; Laughton was considered one of the preeminent stage actors of his day. A tortured homosexual, Laughton found a stalwart friend and supporter in Lanchester in an era when virtually no one was openly gay.

Cancer and Pisces

"But who'll take care of *me?*" The crab and the fish swim in the same element, but have distinctly different emotional responses. Pisces often has a droll or nonstandard response to adversity, which can make super-serious Cancerians completely crazy. Pisces also has an advantage in that they can zone out pretty efficiently with music or a movie or some kind of escapism. But if these two are united, Lord help the person who criticizes the Pisces to the Cancer. In a pinch, Pisces can always seem like the one who needs more protecting, and since that's Cancer's job in the universe . . . well, you have a match made in aqueous heaven.

Scorpio and Scorpio

It's crazy, because these little critters in the wild would just as soon share their sandy burrow with no one, but I've met tons of Scorpios who profess great fondness for their fellow species. They don't necessarily mate with one another ("Okay, you hold your stinger over there, and I'll hold my stinger over here!"), but they share a similar sanguine worldview and don't take each other's rudeness (they'd call it "straight-forwardness") seriously.

Scorpio calls it like they see it, and I once knew a costume designer who staged a Scorpio birthday party event every year. Guests were requested to wear red and black and there were usually enough mates and partners of other elements to add some spice.

One of the most successful partnerships in the history of the American stage was a pair of Scorpios, albeit a pair born at either end of their particular sign. George S. Kaufman (November 17) was a successful, slightly bored, highly neurotic playwright of realistic comedies who had had successful collaborations with others when he met Moss Hart (October 24), who was a generation younger and even more neurotic and unpredictable. Together, the two had an electric relationship when they were alone in a room with a typewriter. Kaufman/Hart pounded out a handful of classic comedies that are still frequently performed today, including *The Man Who Came to Dinner* (based on their mutual friend, radio broadcaster and social stylist Alexander Woolcott) and *You Can't Take it With You*, about an eccentric family.

Scorpio and Pisces

The most famous love relationship in the mid-twentieth century was Elizabeth Taylor (February 27) and Richard Burton (November 10). While their union is not the most ringing endorsement for success of these two signs, it shows emphatically how the power play works out. Both stars were married with children when they collided on the set of *Cleopatra* in 1961. Hitherto, both dominated their particular branches of show business: a rare child-star-turned-ingenue-turned-*femme-fatale*, Taylor had been raised in the protected purlieu of the studio system. Burton had had an impoverished childhood in a Welsh village, and his obvious talent helped a meteoric career rise in the scrappy world of post-World War II British theater.

In the years of their public partnership, the Taylor-Burtons jousted on-and off-screen and electrified the world. They were the first victims of the paparazzi, who followed them from set to set and continent to continent. To make things more interesting, neither star was particularly reticent about their relationship and both were eager to explore the psychological intrigue between them. The projects both were drawn to during their time together (which included marriage and divorce and remarriage and divorce) usually cast Burton as a callous, controlling character (Petruchio in *Taming of the Shrew* and George in *Who's Afraid of Virginia Woolf?*) and Taylor as a masochistic and self-indulgent shrike (Kate in *Shrew* and Martha in *Woolf*). Yet the Taylor-Burtons were far more fascinating (and fabulous) as a tabloid force of nature.

Demi Moore (November 11) and Bruce Willis (March 19) also have that Scorpio/Pisces dynamic, yet neither of them chose to play the public victim once their marriage hit the rocks. Moore's ability to reinvent herself physically, deep into her forties, is another excellent example of Scorpio's determination; the fact that both stars have maintained a friendship after the divorce is a tribute to water signs' ability to adjust and go with the flow.

Pisces and Pisces

These are two signs that *really* understand one another and can communicate by sonar. Enormous mutual inspiration can occur when two fishies collide. Choreographer/dancer Tommy Tune and Bernadette Peters (both February 28) have collaborated on numerous shows together and have enjoyed lengthy Broadway careers and been recognized as experts in their field. No surprise that these two have had remarkable longevity as dancers as well as performers—Pisces rules the feet!

Two Pisces together can also bring out the less-useful aspects of the sign: Pisces are great procrastinators and function best when they have strict deadlines and expectations. Two Pisces cohabitating should definitely have a dishwasher, laundry service, and possibly a maid as well, because there are so many more interesting things to do than fussing with upkeep.

six

MATCHUPS, ALL ASTROLOGICAL NEIGHBORS

You'd think signs that live side by side would have a natural harmony. You'd be right—some of the time. But when you're wrong, anything can happen. What follows is information about how these astrological "neighbors" *really* get along with one another.

The deal with signs next door to one another is that chances are likely that some of the inner planets (Mercury and Venus) will be either in the same sign or in a good relationship to the other person's Sun sign. As these planets influence communication and one's ability to make and be a friend (along with love and beauty), there are huge advantages to being involved with someone whose birthday is right before or after your own.

Aries and Taurus

The ram and the bull may live in the barnyard together but they have their own way of doing things. Taurus likes to think people are with them, while Aries likes to know people will follow them. So there can be the occasional power struggle if Taurus thinks Aries is acting out of line, or being taken advantage of. There can be a similarity of temperament, although Taurus will need more time to flare up and fizzle out.

For impetuous Aries and steadfast Taurus, this can be an enduring if improbable combination. Aries is less likely to dwell on difficulties and more quick to resolve problems. Taurus takes the long road but knows how to plan—in a way that Aries would have neither time nor patience to do. Fiery Aries may be flighty, but there's always a method to their mania. At its best, this sign can be calmed by methodical, rational Taurus. Likewise, if Aries evolves and learns how to avoid quick reactions, they can provide a voice of reason to Taurus, who may need some help learning how to react to uncomfortable situations.

Taurus and Gemini

Earth and air together can be highly natural, or look like one of those film clips from World War II of the invasion of Normandy—nothing but dirt clods being flung into the atmosphere. Watching Taurus and Gemini together can be *quite* a show at its best. As much as Taurus would like to have the upper hand (being, on the face of it, more responsible), Gemini can out-think and out-maneuver Taurus in a New York minute. Yet these two signs can work together well, especially if Gemini appreciates Taurus' qualities of reliability and their overarching aesthetic.

Gemini will invest more energy into relationships than their surroundings, whereas Taurus likes comfort in their environment and will ponder a change of furniture for hours, if not years. Where these signs can be successful is where there's a common interest or activity. Artistic pursuits can be satisfying to both, and if Taurus is one of the more social varieties of bull, this pair can be aces at party planning or organizing a group.

But you'll never mistake a Taurus for a Gemini or vice versa, no matter how much time they spend together. My favorite Taurus/Gemini pair is Bing Crosby (May 2—remember what we said about Taurus and amazing singing) and Bob Hope (May 29). Their film relationship emphasized and developed their astrological personality quirks: Hope always played the hyper-verbal air sign, constantly divided between arrogance and self-doubt, while Crosby was the implacable, smooth, low-key crooner. When these two were in conflict, Crosby invariably came out on top, using earth sign consistency.

Gemini and Cancer

Air and water together can be very exciting for the water sign, as long as Gemini (as we've seen with their relationships with Taurus) is willing to have a period of settling down. Cancer's natural ability to nurture could be thwarted by Gemini's self-sufficiency. The Hollywood power couple of the 1990s exemplified publicly the hazards of these two signs mating. When Gemini Nicole Kidman (June 20) met Cancer Tom Cruise (July 3) and then married him, she did far more adapting than he did. She practiced Scientology, followed him to film sets, and mostly submerged her own career. If you look at the pre-wedding and post-divorce pictures, you'll see a woman completely transformed, both emotionally and (in all likelihood) surgically as well. The roles Kidman has chosen after her divorce showcase a wider range of emotion than she explored in films during the marriage.

But Gemini's unpredictability could go into high gear when faced with a secure Cancer. Because Cancer, as a water sign, is capable of a "go with the flow" philosophy, tolerance for Gemini hijinks and general eccentricities can be greater than others. As long as these two can make each other laugh, they'll be fine. And speaking of comedy, this is a winning combination. Consider Cheech (July 13, a Cancer) and Chong (May 24, an early Gemini). Cheech Marin is in a long line of exasperated and phlegmatic gagmen, while Tommy Chong, the seemingly logical partner, is constantly trying to impose order.

Ultimately, both signs bring their own measure of self-sufficiency and behavioral quirks to any alliance, but it may take Cancer a lifetime to accept Gemini's staccato rhythms of "I'm happy! I'm depressed! I'm bored! When's lunch?" Cancer can impose a stabilizing influence, particularly if Gemini and Cancer meet during some upheaval during Gemini's life, for which Gemini will be grateful.

Cancer and Leo

Side by side are these two signs, yet their differences are acute. Passion can come when water meets fire (steam heat), as well as obliteration of both (too much water on an open flame destroys both fire and water).

The commonalities? Leo can be self-absorbed (okay, egotistical, depending on your vantage point), and Cancer can be self-absorbed (okay, introverted, depending on your vantage). There can be a genuine fascination because both are so different, but Cancer generally has to have a lot of tolerance since Leo can be casual in relations.

Cancer can learn a lot from Leo, not the least of which is to take pride in decisions and impulses, and stand by gut feelings. I've had *many* female Cancer clients through the years and if there's one thing they share, it's the following sentiment: "I need to learn to trust my gut more." To which I say, trust is the start, but then acting on that feeling will get you to the next level of contentment.

Sometimes Cancer can get confused when they're involved with a Leo, since Leo can change focus so quickly. Cancer takes great pride in the nurturing they do while Leo is happy to accept all attention as their due. If this relationship is going to work romantically, Cancer needs to get their ego stroked by the world, not just their feline partner. But this is a couple that can look fabulous together (Mick Jagger, July 26, and Jerry Hall, July 2).

Leo and Virgo

Fire and earth together can produce a substance harder and more durable than either could manage with another element. This is an excellent elemental combination for platonic friends. Leo, for all their need to take charge, sometimes feels their ire is justified if they can vent to a Virgo, who is capable of lengthy analysis. Yet Virgo can be impatient with Leo, who can sometimes make the same mistake or do the same thing over and over. Virgo will note Leo's pride or inability to ask for help; as for their own part, Virgo would just as soon not have *any* help since they can do everything themselves—as long as they have enough time.

As a professional collaboration, these two signs can work incredibly well together. I've had some Leo clients who want to start a business, and when I ask them if they can get a Virgo on board, often they'll say, "I've got a Virgo friend who says they'll help with the bookkeeping." Perfect! Famous Leo/Virgo successful relationships include that of filmmaker Alfred Hitchcock (August 13) who made three successful films with Virgo Ingrid Bergman (August 29): *Spellbound*, *Notorious*, and *Under Capricorn*. As for romance, as long as Virgo can be in the helper role and Leo is getting enough individual attention, there's longevity here.

Virgo and Libra

Again, earth and air can be a low-stress pairing. Libra needs to avoid giving Virgo advice in terms of not taking things seriously or not going off the rails. The joke with Virgo is that they talk about what a bad job they do and how carelessly they do such and such a thing . . . meanwhile everyone around them stands slackjawed in disbelief. Libra's chameleonic side can go into overdrive to the point where scales people are parsing what Virgo says with even *more* precision than what Virgo brings to the conversation. Then again, Libra can help Virgo lighten up, and if Virgo has a showier antic or absurd side (they all do, no matter how hidden), Libra can fan the flames of admiration, inspiring Virgo.

This combo can go wrong in romance. Virgo genius comedian Peter Sellers (September 8) was notorious for his appetite for gorgeous showgirls and had a famous and disastrous marriage with Britt Ekland (October 6). Leaving aside the fact that it's difficult to find *anyone* commenting favorably on the private life of this perfectionistic comic genius, a Libra would be in a constant scramble to be what they *think* Virgo would like them to be.

Libra is chameleonic at times and if they spend a lot of time with a typical Virgo, they can learn habits of precision and perfectionism that are at odds with their basic "whatever" philosophy. Virgo (like Cancer dealing with Gemini) needs to learn that Libra will be more comfortable if not hemmed in. If given an ultimatum of absolutes from a decisive Virgo, Libra could be miserable.

Libra and Scorpio

Direct but deflectable air sign meets sly and strategic water sign. This particular collision is always interesting. Scorpio spends all their time trying to follow what Libra is saying or deciding, Libra wonders why Scorpio can't figure out that they've just changed their mind *again*. Scorpio can be an interesting partner for Libra, partly because of their analytical abilities. Scorpio can also be put into the position of making decisions—just so decisions are being made—which this water sign can find wearying in the long run. Yet Libra has an innate ability and desire to amuse, and if you ever see some of the interviews Truman Capote (September 30) did with intellectual interviewer Dick Cavett (November 19), you'll see two small and intense men highly pleased with their own cleverness.

Just as Libra can derange Virgo by their waffling, Scorpio can learn some habits to protect themselves. These might include cultivating a deliberate mysteriousness or intermittent unavailability while Libra wanders.

Scorpio and Sagittarius

Water and fire together makes what, class? Sagittarius can find Scorpio's strategizing unnecessary and unsociable, while Scorpio may regard Sagittarius as a bit of an impulse freak. Still, these two are so close on the calendar that compensatory planets (such as Mercury and Venus) could help knit them together. Sagittarius has an outdoorsy, athletic side that's simple and basic, while Scorpio has a private side that only gets more pronounced with age. But here's a take from my friend, Scorpio Donna Lethal who was a generous spokeswoman for her sign:

> I think deep down all Scorpios want to be Sagittarians (see Keith Richards). That devil-may-care attitude, the love of good things (Sagittarians have the *best* bathrooms), their lack of worry. We wish we could care so little and have so much fun. You know their ability to coast through life seemingly unscathed? How do they do it? We carry scars for lifetimes.

At its best, Sagittarius can bring out the lightness in Scorpio (or the lightness they aspire to having), while Scorpio can give Sagittarius a reality check when it comes to reading others. Scorpio tends to be skeptical, while Sagittarius can err on the side of being too trusting to the point of gullibility. Sagittarius probably won't change much in their lifetime, but an alliance with a Scorpio or a sign that toes the line for them saves them the trouble of disappointing others by not going along with the party every time.

Sagittarius and Capricorn

Flexible fire and sturdy earth—if these two find one another at the right time of their life, sparks can fly for years. Frank Sinatra (December 12) and Ava Gardner (December 24) married in 1951 and had a volatile relationship. At the time, Sinatra's singing career was in a slump, and since he'd left wife Nancy for this voluptuous *femme fatale*, the tabloids vilified him. However, in a reversal of the usual events, Gardner's career flourished, and in 1953 she was nominated for an Academy Award for *Mogambo*. Her success was such that it was said Sinatra got his Oscar-winning role in *From Here to Eternity* due to her influence. The marriage was stormy, and there were numerous incidents of violence before the pair separated. Yet each retained a passion for the other to the end.

Capricorn can seem very decided about what they want and where they're going and, of the two, is definitely the sign most comfortable with healthy interludes of solitude and consistency. Sagittarius can help get Capricorn out of a rut or be at least willing to have a different perspective. Sagittarius can also be insistent that Capricorn take a break and vary their routine. Since Capricorn often has difficulty self-generating an excuse to take a vacation, Sagittarius can provide a welcome escape valve or be the one who says, "Why don't we . . . ?"

Capricorn and Aquarius

These signs can totally torture each other, even when there's great affection between them. Capricorn is literal-minded; Aquarius likes to improvise. Capricorn does step one, two, three. Aquarius does step three, section B, back to step one, skip ahead to step twenty. Earthy Capricorn can be delighted at Aquarius' imagination and energy, while Aquarius enjoys the encouragement and stability that Capricorn can provide. But these two can very often not be having the same conversation, even when they're the only two in the room. One big truism is that Capricorn will want Aquarius to go for the sure thing while Aquarius, given the choice, will gamble every time.

In my experience, Aquarius is a sign that periodically needs to remove themselves from the world. Capricorn has the same impulse, but for Capricorn it's usually an excuse to work around the clock. Generally, Capricorn is a sign that does what they say they're going to do. Aquarius likes to keep options open and if the Capricorn hears them say, "I'll be over at three o'clock on Sunday," what the Aquarius remembers uttering is "I'll think about calling you on the weekend." Which is to say, just as Capricorn wants to get more precise, Aquarius says, "Don't pen me in!" Both signs have a lot of accepting to do when it comes to the others' quirks and need to be alone.

Aquarius and Pisces

These two signs together follow what I think of as astrological neighborliness. That is—the sign on either side of *your* sign will be someone you have more in common with than you might think. This is partly due to the fact that in all likelihood some of your inner planets, Mercury and/or Venus, could be in compatible signs. If you have Mercury (communication, including writing and yacking and nonverbal messaging) in the same sign, you'll be *simpatico* with communication. If you have Venus (friends, friendliness, attraction, mutuality, empathy, common traits and interests) in the same sign, you'll have soulmate qualities no matter how crazy-different your Sun signs are. And if you've read this far in the book, you probably have an idea of just how different each sign is from the next. Which brings us to one of my favorite Bloomsbury romances: the mutual admiration society of writer/editor Virginia Woolf (January 26) and writer/aesthete Lytton Strachey (March 1).

She was successful in her lifetime, but always had to work very hard at articles, criticisms, and essays as well as keeping the Hogarth Press going. Only after her death did academia take a closer look at Mrs. Woolf and declare her, like Gertrude Stein, a visionary and style-setter. This should be no surprise to fans of Aquarius, that independent air sign. Yet Woolf took an exceptionally long time to develop her skills.

Virginia Stephens grew up in a rarified and intellectual late-Victorian household, and only through personal calamities (the death of mother and father in quick succession) were she and surviving siblings, including sister Vanessa, able to live independently—highly unusual for young unmarried women in that era. Enter Oxford friend Lytton Strachey, who had been attached to brother Thoby at university. Thoby's tragic death in World War I put these two bright lights together and their relationship was mutually productive and beneficial as well as intellectually interesting. Strachey made his name with a series of profiles, which were basically reappraisals of Victorian-era celebrities, and always had a passionate interest in the visual arts (a water sign interest). Young Virginia was charmed by his quick wit and lively mind as well as his complete disregard for convention. Scratch the surface—sometimes you have to dig—and you will find that all Aquarians are rebels at heart. Strachey was highly sensitive and brittle; he and Virginia were so besotted with one another they actually considered marriage for a time.

Here are some other pairs linked together by chance, circumstance and now history: Boris Spasky, January 30, and Bobby Fischer, March 9; *Alice in Wonderland* creator Lewis Carroll, January 27, and illustrator John Tenniel, February 28.

Pisces and Aries

These two signs straddle a magical time of the year. Since the zodiac begins with Aries, we have a sign concerned with endings, nostalgia, and things hidden or concealed (accidentally and on purpose) linked to a sign that's about renewal, zest, and fresh starts. As with Capricorn and Aquarius, these two signs would seem to have little in common, but my field experience suggests that Pisces can be inspired by Aries' energy, while Aries is impressed by Pisces soulfulness. I knew two women who were best friends throughout college and their friendship actually led them to some very prestigious Ivy League jobs. The Aries applied for a teaching position first, of course, and then encouraged her Pisces friend to apply. Neither of them could have afforded to live in the pricey Ivy League town on their own; since there was a bit of culture shock, they were grateful to have one another for support.

As for romance with these two signs, Aries sometimes is cast in the role of the instigator or encourager, while Pisces, once smitten and committed, is usually more stable than Aries.

Pisces, with their natural flair for art, music, poetry, or chronically siding with the underdog (or being an underdog as a self-defense mechanism) is more mysterious to Aries than Aries, with their straightforward, confident manner, is to Pisces. Each sign has a trait that fascinates the other; each sign sees something in the other that is lovable yet unfathomable.

seven

ASTRO-ELEMENTAL
OPPOSITES

Opposites attract—wouldn't you agree? In millenia past, the earliest star-gazers apportioned each of the four elements to a particular gender. So fire and air are masculine; earth and water are feminine. But that means that the oppositions (which are fire and air and earth and water) are *both* the same gender. This adds an element of harmony and compatibility for gay couples, who share a gender. For heterosexual pairings, this means one party will have a Sun sign opposite their gender.

For example, Cancer women can be ultrafeminine, having an impulse to nurture and grow. Cancer males can have the sensitivity without having any way to remove themselves from the fray, emotionally speaking that is. The opposite sign, Capricorn, is an earth sign, also considered feminine. So a female Capricorn will have the determination and independence that in many males is solitude and possible tendencies to depression. If you have a Cancer/Capricorn relationship, where the male is the Cancer and the woman is the Capricorn, the female Capricorn may be the one who calls the shots, or is in a position of constantly urging the Cancer male to get over things, either by direct comment or example.

In terms of endurance, opposites that attract one another can definitely go the distance—even as they defy others' expectations and dire predictions. Sometimes the "opposites attract" combo can have a certain shelf-life. Read "Important Astrological Terms" at the end of this book, which defines these intervals in greater depth. Also, another factor to bear in mind is that when transiting planets are making difficult angles (e.g., a square) to one of these signs, due to the nature of geometry as exerted on a 360-degree circle, the other sign also experiences that square. In short, when one sign is stressed, so is the other: no one gets a break at the same time.

Aries and Libra

Potentially lethal, but professionally advantageous. These two signs are an amusing-to-onlookers example of how opposites attract. Impetuous Aries has peculiar chemistry with diffident, dallying Libra. Yet Libra can help Aries focus—or at least be consistent in their efforts, which isn't always the best thing for those involved. The ram is all about moving forward, but Libra likes to spend time considering. Aries and Libra can also be a successful but highly short-term pairing. Sparks usually fly right away, and given the choice of the other cardinal signs (including Cancer and Capricorn), Aries usually chooses Libra, who'll give them no argument or require special handling. I was amused to find a variety of intense Aries/Libra relationships once I started researching, and in all of these cases, the Aries was the instigator, while the Libra was the agent acted upon, the victim, or the willing enabler. Take the case of the poet Verlaine (March 30) and his dear friend, poet Arthur Rimbaud (October 20). These two were brilliant young men of letters in France, penning the equivalent of chart-topping number one hits in poetry . . . until Verlaine got drunk and shot Arthur.

How about my favorite silent movie star, Buster Keaton (October 4), who began his film career as a nonreactive, skinny, and gymnastic counterpart to America's favorite funnyman, Fatty Arbuckle (March 24)? Fatty was a huge (in every sense) star when he was matched with Buster, who always remembered his friend's kindness, particularly after Fatty was accused of the murder of party girl Virginia Rappe and stood trial. Though Fatty was acquitted, only loyal Buster would give him work after that, directing his films. Of course Fatty couldn't use his own name—instead choosing an inside-joke alias: Will B. Good.

The pair that loved together and worked together were those thrill-seeking tabloid criminals of the 1930s, Clyde Barrow (March 24) and Bonnie Parker (October 1). Their bloody crime spree encompassed five Midwestern states and included the homicides of nine police officers. During their lives and particularly after death, these two have been celebrated as a pair of star-crossed criminals.

In all three cases, we see that Aries basically takes the initiative, leaving Libra to either clean up or suffer the consequences of the relationship.

Taurus and Scorpio

Both fixed signs (meaning "fixed in their ways"), Taurus and Scorpio can have remarkably similar behaviors when in one another's company. Taurus likes to get into a groove and do things consistently, which Scorpio definitely understands. Scorpio tends to keep things hidden, while Taurus likes to present themselves as the honest broker who keeps everything aboveboard. Both signs can be verbally blunt in a way that leaves others saying, "Hey, what did they mean by *that*?" but both signs are sincere in their having everyone's best interests at heart.

In terms of stubbornness—Taurus wins. In terms of resistance, Scorpio prevails. Taurus will be asking, "What did I say?" while Scorpio embarks on what turns into a two-year silent-treatment campaign. Both signs can come together on projects involving nurturing, particularly gardening. Taurus and Scorpio can be fiercely loyal to one another, even as they view one another as exotic creatures needing a special habitat. If you're one sign or the other, and are interested in your opposite, suggest attending a botanical garden or garden show. You'll find plenty to agree about—and lots to learn from one another.

Gemini and Sagittarius

Each can be quick-witted and Gemini's brittleness can be offset by Sagittarius' ability to process and move on. This is a powerful alliance, one that can get others excited. Sagittarius is a flexible fire sign that needs to spend a lot of time outdoors or in a variety of activities, and Gemini is a flexible air sign that needs a lot of intellectual stimulation. Sagittarius can think in broad strokes, while Gemini can think in broad strokes *and* get caught up in details. As a romantic pairing, this can be successful, but only if both parties have attained a certain level of maturity. Sagittarius hates to be hemmed in, and Gemini will get bored quickly. These two can definitely provide enough excitement and unpredictability to keep life interesting for the other.

A successful literary/romantic pairing was Joan Didion (December 5) and John Gregory Dunne (May 25). Didion was considered the more high-brow author for her personal essays and social commentary, while Dunne was more descriptive and dramatic in his work. Yet the two collaborated successfully as script doctors for a number of years. Since Dunne's passing, Didion's grieving period has included a memoir on becoming a widow, *The Year of Magical Thinking,* later turned into a successful stage play. What's interesting about this pair is that Dunne definitely took on some Sagittarian elements as a writer (antic adventures for his characters and an overwhelming sense of what's "fair"), while Didion became more Gemini in her perspective—alert to myriad possibilities and highly, precisely verbal.

Cancer and Capricorn

Of all the oppositions I've seen through the years, this one can be the most amusing to those of us looking on. The watery, emotional, boundary-hating side of Cancer can turn to ice or steam when in the presence of straight-talking Capricorn. Siblings born eighteen months apart (a popular age-span) whose birthdays fall in these signs will always be completely different, and perplexing to one another. Yet, there is something for both of these folks to learn. Cancer can benefit from a lot of outside structure imposed upon them and, if they are around someone who is organized and list-making like Capricorn, it can have a beneficial effect. Capricorn sometimes needs help interpreting others' emotions, which Cancer is excellent at doing.

Not so long ago, I had the opportunity to have a conversation with a full-on Capricorn scientist, the mom of a Cancer daughter. I explained that her daughter would be loyal to her friends *unto death*, and didn't have the same need for solitude that the mom did. There was a certain amount of drama and analysis her daughter would need to do as she maneuvered through middle school, coming into adulthood. Both Cancer and Capricorn are capable of spending long stretches of time in solitude, and both signs have strong leadership abilities. Capricorn, as an earth sign, is naturally predisposed towards intellectual analysis versus Cancer's spectacular insights into emotional affect. Both signs can stick to their guns for no good reason, and if they're at loggerheads, chances are it'll be the Cancer who'll decide to compromise or change the subject sufficiently.

Cancer can be inspirational for Capricorn, and the example that I like to cite is Capricorn Howard Hughes (December 24), who was enamored with Cancer actress Jane Russell (June 21). Their partnership produced an enduring piece of technology, love it or hate it: the underwire bra. Hughes, an aircraft engineer, technician and inventor constructed the first-ever lingerie to lift a lady's bosom. Ironically, Russell never wore Hughes' invention, but he is credited for the design. And if you watched television during the seventies, you may recall Russell's stint as a pitchwoman for Playtex "Cross-Your-Heart bras, for us full-figured gals."

Leo and Aquarius

Opposites attract, up to a point. Leo's egomania is something that blithe and distracted Aquarius could easily overlook. As I've written, I see Leo and Aquarius' neighbor (Capricorn) much more often. Aquarius is a quirky and clubbable sign, and a Leo who meets someone who's *not* impressed with them—well now, that's intriguing! I was amused to research some of the muses for literary lion George Bernard Shaw, a man whose writing career began in the Victorian age and lived to see the invention and deployment of the atomic bomb.

One glorious partnership on-screen was that of Robert Redford (August 18) and Paul Newman (January 26), who were first teamed up in *Butch Cassidy and the Sundance Kid.* Both performers exemplified a particular style of low-key masculine American cool that was the antithesis of the previous generation of male stars. Redford's brooding affect coupled with Newman's crackling intelligence made moviegoers of all ages and genders swoon. The pair teamed up again in 1975 for *The Sting,* and this time, they got to keep the money and live.

In the "strange bedfellows" department, we find Aquarian actor Vanessa Redgrave (January 30) allying with Leo dictator/rogue statesman Yasser Arafat (August 4). Not surprisingly, the Leo in the equation only had his luster burnished, while the Aquarian's reputation suffered. Despite Redgrave's eloquent argument against war and displacement camps, the world took her sympathies as a full-on endorsement of PLO methods and, like Jane Fonda before her, she found that most of her critics in the developed world couldn't really analyze her motives without presuming the worst. Fortunately, both Aquarius and Leo can be oblivious to the reactions of others.

Virgo and Pisces

Both signs need to have some serious relationship time with people of other elements, persuasions, and even genders. Pisces is a dreamer and Virgo is highly practical. Ask a Virgo how often their dreams revolve around them organizing a closet or cleaning out a room or reprogramming a computer. Pisces is also resistant to being changed and Virgo sometimes thrives on a challenge. Just as with the other oppositions, these natal positions mean that when times are tough for one, they'll be tough for the other as well.

I can think of two girlfriends who had these Sun signs who were a dynamic combination for seven years. They lived in southern California, the most therapeutically minded state in the union, and Virginia, the Virgo, was an honest-to-gosh colonic irrigation specialist. That meant her job involved cleaning out the part of the body ruled by her sign. She was highly health conscious and totally involved with her companion, Patti, the Pisces, a musician who welcomed a certain degree of caretaking. Aside from a certain amount of bossiness from Virginia and grumbling compliance on Patti's part, they were perfectly compatible: one huge factor may have been their completely opposite schedules (both worked nine to five, but it was A.M. to P.M. for Virginia, and P.M. to A.M. for Patti). However, the time came when a difficult period arose for both (see first paragraph) and both craved freedom at the same time. Now they're friends, and are amazed that they ever were lovers.

Kelly, another Pisces, also has excellent relations with a Virgo—partly because of her appreciation of their unique talents: "I get along great with Virgos. My first boyfriend was a Virgo, my dad's a Virgo, I have good Virgo friends. I admire their organization and they seem to be patient with my attempts to get them to be a little more fun . . . and my occasional irrationality."

eight

MATCHUPS, ALL ELEMENT COMBINATIONS

Fire, Earth, Air, and Water

Just the basics, mixed together!

Okay, you've read about what happens when like meets like. What happens when we mix it up? This section explores the myriad results of combined elements. You don't need to be a chemist to understand this, but bear in mind the basics when it comes to each element. Here's a cheat sheet to get you started!

We're going to get into greater detail. For some of these combinations, the number of famous folks I could reference was overwhelming. However, just because some of these combinations may be more challenging doesn't mean the relationship isn't successful or enduring. Please look in the "Matchups, Neighboring Signs" chapter for more combinations.

Fire Plus Earth

These two can create a relationship that's hard and enduring (like ceramics), or hard and brittle (also like ceramics). Sometimes there's real personal growth involved on part of both parties because the nature of both is so different. "Lighten up," says the fire sign. "But then I'm not prepared!" responds the earth sign. Fire and earth can have wildly varying characteristics, and I've certainly seen stubborn fire signs (like Leo) have enduring relationships with easily-swayed earth signs (Virgo—yes, sometimes!). Ambition can be a place where both signs dwell happily.

Aries and Virgo

An interesting, unlikely pairing, Aries' go-go-go forward motion contrasts with Virgo's reflective or analytical side. In my practice, I don't see this relationship as having particular endurance, but there are some stellar examples of collaborations that really changed the cultural landscape. Genius choreographer Merce Cunningham (April 16) and minimalist avatar/genius composer John Cage (September 5) come to mind. When they met, each was a struggling artist. Together they assembled perhaps the most revolutionary dance company that ever existed. Cage's ideas about rhythm, silence, and "prepared" pianos were the perfect complement to Cunningham's raw, body-conscious movements. Respect was mutual, but it was Cage the Virgo who took over the company's management and marketing reins—he also planned their road trips. When working with fire, air, or water, count on Virgo always—*always*—to be the organized one.

Aries and Capricorn

The ram and the goat. One climbs the mountain and the other ... climbs the mountain. Aries can lighten up Capricorn like nobody's business and Capricorn can stabilize the ram. Caps can spend their time figuring out how to make Aries' schemes work. Though these signs are ninety degrees away and therefore "square" to one another (see "Important Astrological Terms" on page 193), that built-in tension can become passion, given the right mix of personalities. These two will have tension during the same times of the year: midsummer and autumn, and should be patient with the other's foibles then.

Leo and Taurus

The lion and the bull can be formidable rivals and adversaries and really have to work hard if they want to get anywhere. Interestingly, their relationship can be mutually beneficial because of the rivalry. A Taurus is capable of ignoring the lion's roar, and sometimes takes the position of guiding the king of the jungle. Think of the circus analogy: someone has to wake the lion, get it in the ring, get it to roar and perform, and then get it back in the cage without bloodshed and mayhem. Taurus has a steady hand, and as long as these folks respect a lion's pride (self esteem, versus family group, although both apply!), this can be a relationship where each respects the other's talents.

Leo and Capricorn

See "Leo and Capricorn" in the chapter on fire signs. These two signs are one of my "classic" pairs and go together like cats and cream . . . or is that *chèvre?*

Sagittarius and Taurus

Look no further than Marx (May 5) and Engels (November 28). I was rattling my records to see if I could find a good example of a successful partnership, and lo and behold: the world's most influential social manifesto writers show what happens when the Taurean understanding of materialism coincides with Sagittarian high-minded social justice. These two signs are *so* different that it makes sense they could interact.

Sagittarius has that risk-taking tendency, and Taurus could definitely be inspired by Sagittarius' willingness to toss out the rules and start fresh. Oh, but here's another pairing that may not have global impact, but in its day, was highly amusing to pop culture audiences: Cher (May 20) and Gregg Allman (December 7). After the death of older brother Duane, Gregg was disconsolate and hell-bent on rock star self-destruction. Enter Cher, who since girlhood, had been in thrall to visionary manager/husband Sonny Bono, an unusually possessive Aquarius. She was definitely ready to run her own life, so why not someone else's besides? Musically, she couldn't have found a more interesting contrast to Sonny, whose pop sensibility was always aimed at the bottom line. Gregg came from the blueshouse grind tradition of swamp rock and must have seemed thoroughly dangerous and potentially redeemable. The result? Suffice to say, we all know how stubborn Taurus can be when pushed—or pulled.

Sagittarius and Virgo

This is another pairing where the signs are ninety degrees apart (a square). Sagittarius' wild side can definitely come to the fore when these two collide. Virgo's tendency to fuss and bustle can be front and center when confronted with Sagittarius' accident-prone side. Advantages: Virgo's willingness to explore new vitamins and remedies will have a willing customer in Sagittarius. Disadvantages: Sagittarius' impulsiveness can make Virgo's digestion really, really uncomfortable. There is good news, however; these people can learn to accommodate one another—eventually. Sadge can lighten up Virgo and the maiden can organize the archer's life in a pleasurable way.

Fire Plus Air

Together, this can be a dynamic combination in work and love. Each partner brings energy and enthusiasm to the table. The trick is making sure someone can do the follow-through or read the fine print. Air and fire signs together can complement strengths and appreciate the aspects of the other that are either not a priority, or not possible. "A little wind kindles; much puts out the fire," in the words of George Herbert.

Aries and Gemini

This is a potentially electric pairing as Aries and Gemini energy can be similar, compatible, and utterly exhausting for those around them. A conversation between these two can be a chatter-fest that goes from 90 to 200 mph and then abruptly stops as both run out of gas at the same time. Aries sometimes has a hard time perceiving Gemini's dual personality tendencies. Geminis can be frustrated if they don't think an Aries is picking up on all the subtleties of a situation. Gemini is fascinated by analyzing others whereas Aries has limited time, ability, and aptitude for such exercises. A ram would much rather be doing. Under the right circumstances, Aries and Gemini can make magic happen. James Watson (April 6) and Francis Crick (June 8) made history by discovering the double helix in 1953. Watson, younger than Crick by twelve years was a brilliant American student with a Ph.D. at 22. Crick was a brilliant biophysicist who didn't have his doctorate yet. The two of them collaborated on work done by biologists and physicists and figured out the physical structure of DNA, the double helix. "We didn't leave it that Jim did the biology and I did the physics," Crick explained. "We both did it together and switched roles and criticized each other." With two bright and motivated personalities working at full tilt, there's enough work for all, thus turf wars are avoided.

Another interesting ram/twin connection is between longtime perennial bachelor/satyr Warren Beatty (March 30) and Annette Benning

(May 29). Beatty had long made a habit of bedding leading ladies or finding parts for his girlfriends Julie Christie (April 14, *McCabe and Mrs. Miller, Shampoo*) and Diane Keaton (January 5, *Reds*), but wasn't ready to settle down until hitting his fifties. I would conjecture that having an older Taurus sister in Shirley MacLaine set the tone for his fondness for independent, resolute female partners. So far, the Beatty/Benning partnership has been stable.

Aries and Aquarius

Here's another superficially harmonious combination. These signs are sixty degrees apart and share energy, initiative, curiosity, and fearlessness. They can also bring out the best in one another, but Aries will want to dominate. This can bring out the "la-dee-dah, I don't care" side of Aquarius, and the water-carrier's main recourse is to thoroughly change direction, perplexing the by-the-rules Aries.

When Bob Woodward (March 26) and Carl Bernstein (February 14) were assigned by *The Washington Post* to cover a quirky crime story—a break-in at the Watergate Hotel—they had little in common. Woodward was a straight-arrow, ex-military man patiently pulling assignments in the newsroom. Bernstein was a cocky and stylish feature writer who defied the era's custom by wearing his hair nearly at hippie-length. Together, the two of them found there were more twists and turns in the break-in story once the burglars could be connected to members of the Republican ruling elite. And, unlike many collaborations that can quickly get competitive (and fizzle out), these two had complementary working habits and soon their bylines were linked forever. Their collaboration extended for many years and is one of the models for modern investigative journalism.

Leo and Gemini

There's a harmonious angle between these two signs. Leo enjoys a certain amount of homage, and Gemini may (or may not) be up for providing this. Leo can be a highly protective sign, and since Gemini can be flaky (okay, quirky and unpredictable), the nurturing side of the lion can have full expression here. Leo can also have a childish side that comes out with Gemini (two personalities in one, remember) and pride can easily transform to petulance. In work relationships, this can translate to a dynamic sales/marketing team, or manager/utility player relationship. These two are also exciting for others to be around.

Leo and Libra

Fire and air will always have something to say to one another, and my money says Leo trumps Libra. Yet, both signs have a strong aesthetic sense and can be great friends and supports for each another, bringing out a side the other hasn't fully developed. Christopher Dean (July 27) and Jayne Torvill (October 7) seemed like a long-shot in the 1984 Olympics. Their specialty, ice dancing, was a crowd-pleaser but wasn't considered on the same caliber as the other winter sports. In spite of that, these two transfixed the world with their partnership on Ravel's *Bolero*. Torvill's balance and Dean's strength made for a 24-karat Olympic event.

Sagittarius and Libra

Sagittarius likes to have an audience sometimes, and Libra is usually happy to defer to other signs that want to make a big noise, so this can be a fun combination as long as neither partner craves stability or consistency. Sagittarius can be a sign that really lightens up others. Since Libra's scales sometimes swing back and forth, it's helpful for them to know someone who isn't as bedeviled with a plethora of choices as they.

Sagittarius and Aquarius

Both are risk-takers, both hate to be hemmed in, and both are independent. Although Sagittarius tends to collect motley groups of people,

Aquarius prefers to drift from social scene to social scene. Conventional astrology says this is a fine match because the two signs are sixty degrees apart. However, for these two to get traction with one another—with the independent impulses in each—it's a bit of a long shot. On some level, both signs crave stability and someone to rebel against.

Fire Plus Water

In tandem, these folks can be exciting and productive (think of how the steam engine revolutionized the western economy) or a big fizzle. In a version of "Paper, rock, scissors," a water sign can cancel out the fire quickly, but over time, the fire sign can transform the water sign into invisible steam. Cancer and Aries can be a successful relationship (with a LOT of accommodation on Cancer's part)—so can Pisces and Aries, or Pisces and Sagittarius. Scorpio is the one water sign that is a very peculiar fit to its fire sign counterparts.

Aries and Cancer

These signs are ninety degrees apart, making that awkward "square" angle that can create conflict. Both signs are at the start of a season—spring and summer. Fire is outward, water is inward. The ram climbs the mountain, the crab stays close to the sea and prefers to remain unseen. Aries is young, Cancer likes to nurture. Aries has energy, Cancer wants to resist energy. In my professional experience, when I have a Cancer female who's talking about being interested in an Aries, I am *always* careful to outline the sign's parameters and the fact that Cancer needs to have the thickest of shells at times with this particular sun sign. Yet Aries and Cancer can push one another in way that surprise both. Historically, a thoroughly successful partnership was teacher Annie Sullivan (April 14) and blind/deaf/mute Helen Keller (June 27). When they met, Annie was a poor, half-blind Irish immigrant who'd spent her youth at the Perkins Institution in Massachusetts. She needed a job and the southern Keller family needed someone to mind their child, who'd been disabled by scarlet fever. This story is best told in playwright William Gibson's drama, *The Miracle Worker* but the essence of it is that the Aries in this case was not going to let the Cancer get away with anything, and the Cancer was actually craving sensation. Wouldn't you know it, Annie and Helen were lifelong companions forever after.

Aries and Scorpio

If you've been browsing some of the other quirky combos, like Leo/Capricorn, or Sagittarius/Taurus, you'll have a sense of what these two have in common (not much). These are two signs that can drive each other completely around the bend yet retain a mutual affection. What's missing from the combination? Patience. Aries' impulsiveness is at odds with Scorpio's strategizing. Scorpio's secretiveness is completely incomprehensible to straight-ahead, call-them-as-they-see-them Aries sincerity. Dudley Moore (April 19) and Peter Cook (November 17) were different in background, affect, sensibility, and character, yet were the breakout stars from 1960s satirical troupe *Beyond the Fringe*. When you look at these two as a pair, Scorpio will seem more scheming than usual, and Aries more childlike.

Aries and Pisces

The first and last signs together can get together if some event brings them in proximity but it will take a certain amount of delicacy and tolerance on Pisces' part and a lot of patience on Aries' part. I've known roommate situations between these two signs that started off very positively and ended in a stage of indifference, mostly due to expectations. Pisces generally needs some coaxing—which Aries can do—but Aries generally can't do as much coaxing as Pisces craves. If Pisces feels cut off, resentment can build. I have *never* known a Pisces who can confront another calmly and say "That really bugged me." Venomous unsent emails and much blabbing to third parties, yes, but not direct confrontation!

Leo and Scorpio

There is so much to say about this combination—I can't wait to explore in greater detail. To begin, let's pick six newsmakers:

Bill (August 19) and Hillary Clinton (October 26)

Arnold (July 30) and Maria Schwarzenegger (November 6)

Ted Hughes (August 17) and Sylvia Plath (October 27)

Here, the men in these pairings are definitely the beasts that roared, while their partners all exemplify Scorpio's stoic, secretive, surprisingly sensual tendencies. In the case of Bill Clinton we learn more about him when considering his emotional fidelity to his steadier Scorpio. Leo needs a long leash, it's true, but they also welcome Scorpio's practical nature. Bill Clinton's political ascendancy in Arkansas was bankrolled at the very beginning by Hillary's high-paying corporate law job. Scorpio tends to be more business-like and more organized. It was Hillary who was vilified for the Whitewater real estate deal—not Leo Bill. In the case of the Schwarzaneggar marriage, reporters who have covered the couple together report that Maria is diligent about keeping Arnold on track and on message where digressions would otherwise come easily.

The case of Leo Ted Hughes and Scorpio Sylvia Plath was much unhappier unless you take into consideration the fact that these two poets basically have an immortal story in the literature of the twentieth century. Sylvia was not a typical Scorpio save for the secretive suicide attempts. Her outward ambition seemed much more fiery than her yearning for domestic tranquility. Her diaries and notebooks are packed with references to improving her cooking, cleaning, and other housewife-y skills. So what went wrong? Astrologically speaking, she had some big planets working against her in February, 1963 when she succeeded in killing herself (a Jupiter opposition being the most disastrous). In her chart, she also had Mars in Leo; Mars in a heterosexual woman's chart is a fabulous indicator for the type of man she finds appealing. Mars had moved into Leo that month which emboldened her in whatever endeavor she would have tried. We all know the poems for *Ariel* were arranged on her desk, many of which had been written in the previous six weeks when she moved herself and her two children into another apartment. She had been working hard on the work that mattered to her and numerous accounts suggest she had hopes of being rescued from herself.

Leo and Pisces

Sizzle, sizzle, pop! I'm always curious to see how each of these signs in combination with one another can take on the other's attributes. Example: Lucille Ball (Aug. 6) and Desi Arnaz (Mar. 2) had onscreen personalities that were the opposite of what you'd think. Lucy was the dithering, dreamy, befuddled romantic, while husband "Ricky Ricardo" was the smooth, suave bandleader (another fabulous Leo occupation). He was in the spotlight—she yearned to share it. Behind the scenes, Lucille Ball took the reins, insisting she have her own Cuban-born husband portray her TV mate. Other interracial partnerships came decades later, but for the early 1950s, a Spanish/Scottish pairing was revolutionary. And— because of the genius of the show's writers and the performances—it was a first for television.

But don't think Leo will always be the dominant player in this combo. The most famous marital bust-up of the mid-century was Eddie Fisher (Aug 10) leaving Aries cinema sweetheart Debbie Reynolds (April 1), for Elizabeth Taylor (February 27), and then himself being discarded when Liz met Dick (Burton, November 10). In this case, Scorpio's ability to strategize and maneuver definitely prevailed over Leo's assertiveness.

Sagittarius and Cancer

Another electric partnership, and one that can exhaust both parties in the case of blood relations. George VI (December 14) and older brother Edward VIII (better known as the Duke of Windsor, June 23) were cordial during their lifetimes despite having extreme temperament and lifestyle differences. Edward was stylish and brought a breezy informality to royal public relations in the 1920s, even giving his name to a new style of cravat, the Windsor knot. George, the younger brother, was an athlete and happily married to the only woman he loved. Embarrassed by his stammer, he was happy staying out of public view. But when witty and outspoken golden prince Edward met twice-married Wallis Warfield Simpson (June 19), all of his Cancerian needs (to be nurtured, to have a home) were awakened. The result was a historic abdication, that provided Britain with the right king at the right time.

Sagittarius and Pisces

You've been reading this book and should have a basic understanding of how the elements work temperamentally and dynamically. If not, just think about the images. Look, there's Pisces, two fishies swimming in opposite directions. There on the riverbank is a centaur, arrow nocked and drawn, his aim steady. Who do *you* think is in charge in this ménage?

A wise Pisces will go with the flow and let the Sagittarius shoot the arrows at moving water. If the Sagittarius is particularly impulsive or headstrong, Pisces can comfortably take on the role of sounding board or wise counselor.

Earth Plus Air

A fun, if maddening (to the earth sign) pairing. Air sign folks tend not to let things seep in while earth is all about absorbing, brooding, reflecting, and perhaps eventually responding. Air people often like to have earth sign friends for their stabilizing effects, while earth people can be inspired by air sign fearlessness and disregard for consequences. Earth sign people can stabilize air sign people. They don't always listen to one another and so half-made plans can make for missed appointments or opportunities. Earth sign people will usually "bail out" your air sign friend, whereas the air sign person will always be able to see the lighter side, or the "fixable" aspects of some problem earth sign people are having.

Taurus and Libra

Madonna's song, "Material Girl" sums up the best aspects of this relationship. Both Taurus (earth) and Libra (air) are ruled by Venus. This planet's focus is love, beauty, friendship, relationships, romance, and, interestingly enough, a responsiveness to aesthetics. Taurus can be stubborn, Libra can be wishy-washy, but where these two agree is on some artistic or material object or experience. Oohing and aahing over decorative arts or aesthetic experiences is a way for these two to find a separate peace. Libra can be helpful to Taurus who tends to experience the world in a my-way-or-the-highway philosophy, while Taurus can be useful to Libra with consistency and earnestness.

Taurus and Aquarius

This is another painful, awkward encounter that can ignite like wildfire (if the Aquarian is sufficiently motivated). Taurus' natural stubbornness and recessive nature gets a real workout from forward-looking Aquarius. This is another match that can mystify onlookers, but makes enough sense to the participants to have its own momentum. I've always loved that Sonny Bono was an Aquarian, and that his television career with his genius wife Cherlynn Sarkisian Bono (May 20) turned her into the clotheshorse of the post-Hippie era. One visionary plus one practical thinker equals very creative activities.

Virgo and Gemini

Take Gemini's breathless curiosity and impetuousness and marry it to Virgo's painstaking perfectionism. Or, take Gemini's roaming proclivities and try to blend with Virgo's managerial side. Virgo sometimes needs reassurance, and if there's anything Gemini has in abundance, it's the ability to talk anyone into anything. As long as Gemini can be patient with Virgo's need to go at their own pace and Virgo doesn't get too frustrated with Gemini's will-o'-the-wisp staying power, these two signs can certainly have a dynamic interaction. See the earth elements chapter, Virgo entry for more on this combination.

Virgo and Aquarius

This is very, very strange and can be a recipe for romantic disaster for the Virgo who doesn't fully grasp Aquarius's self-proclaimed need to do exactly what they want, when they want. Aquarians born very close to January are sometimes a better fit for Virgins; ditto Virgins born at the end of their sign in September, who can have a capriciousness similar to Aquarius.

Capricorn and Gemini

Capricorn forgives Gemini anything. Gemini realizes Capricorn is thoroughly reliable, and will also be willing to take responsibility. Capricorn takes responsibility, realizes Gemini has moved onto something new ... and on it goes. This can be an excellent relationship in an office setting, but Gemini should be close to Taurus (or Cancer) and have some personal stability to appreciate the nuances of Capricorn consistency.

Capricorn and Libra

Another square, this is not a natural fit but I've seen it work with friendships. Capricorn is incredibly independent, Libra is social. Capricorn will only see one side, Libra insists on seeing more than one. Capricorn is fun to "jolly" and Libra is fun to take care of. This is a win-win situation if both signs really see each other clearly. This is also a relationship where both parties can agree on a project that helps or assists a third party. Because Capricorn and Libra are both cardinal signs, they're pretty directed but they can learn from one another.

Earth Plus Water

This combination can be fertile and successful. Think of the rain needed to grow the plants in a garden. Think of wet clay that can be molded into any form, useful or decorative. Think of the fun you had as a kid playing at the water's edge at the beach, or in a mud puddle. Whoops, did I write "mud"? The downside to the earth/water combination can be a mutually chronically sludgy temperament. Earth and Water signs together can be—periodically and metaphorically—emotionally "stuck in the mud" if other factors aren't successful. There is a natural advantage to many earth/water combinations which have to do with the geometry of the signs. Earth signs are 60 degrees apart from two out of the three water signs.

Taurus and Cancer

Harmony, compatibility, and mutual understanding characterize this combination. Though they were never romantically linked, hoofer Fred Astaire (May 10) and his stylish blonde partner Ginger Rogers (July 16) had plenty of compatibility, and more importantly, together added up to something incandescent. However, let us not forget that the bull and the crab together can stick to their guns in a way that leaves little maneuvering. Cancer sometimes gets more creative with sideways movements to circumvent Taurean stubbornness.

Taurus and Pisces

This is a passionate and fruitful relationship, although not in the way you might expect. Take the dominant pair of the British rock band, The Who. Songwriter/guitarist Pete Townshend (May 19) has long has an embattled but productive relationship with frontman Roger Daltrey (March 1). Townshend, with his beaky visage and awkward stance is the muscle behind the flash of Daltrey, who has been making fans swoon since the first Mods. This is super for an artistic relationship if you're a Taurus or Pisces collaborating with your opposite number. Pisces is concerned with art, music, song, and escapism, while Taurus is the down-to-business person who keeps the train running. In his prime, Daltrey had an immensely powerful voice with a distinctive range, and one rock critic commented long ago that the handsome singer was merely the embodiment of the bloke playing guitar behind him.

Virgo and Cancer

Another compatible mix—the earthiness of Virgo can help Cancer defuse over-the-top emotional responses. Remember, earth plus water can be a fertile soil for all kinds of blooms. And though we never think of them as having a professional relationship (their careers took such different paths), Academy Award-winning actor Anne Bancroft (September 17) and longtime hubby filmmaker/comedian Mel Brooks (June 28) had a long and harmonious partnership. Bancroft had a cool and analytical side but she also had the Meditteranean passion that came with many first generation Italian-Americans. Brooks' career had several milestones, including his emergence as an energetic and imaginative gag writer on *Your Show of Shows* and his droll and artistically adventurous partnership with Carl Reiner as the 2000 Year Old Man.

Virgo and Scorpio

The million-dollar question for these two is: *Qui es mas picky?* Others perceive both Virgo and Scorpio going through life with a magnifying glass, looking for flaws. Virgo and Scorpio usually believe their acumen is completely justified. Virgo can be filled with self-doubt—aiming for impossible perfection. Scorpio aims for perfection, and can be heedless to others. Who is more critical? My good friend Donna Lethal, an early Scorpio, sums up this relationship:

> I am torn: I would like to have [Virgo's] ability to organize, what with the multi-colored day planners and calendars and meticulous Facebook updating and texting. On the other hand, I hate being treated like *I'm* on the checklist: "Lunch with Scorpio. Check." Being an item on the list to be crossed off next is annoying. I had a Virgo pal who got addicted to Adderall; our friendship ended. If there is anyone who does *not* need "extra help" to focus, it's a Virgo. The word "spontaneity" is not in their vocabulary so don't try to do things "on the fly" or surprise them with a party. I have a sneaking suspicion that my Virgo gal pals had their babies by meticulous planning—if anyone has the ability to mechanically mess with their biological clock, it's a Virgo. . . . I did date a Virgo man once, though, and he was nothing like a Virgo at all. He was balanced by a Cancer moon, so he was very emotional. We're still friends and he's great at fixing things and like all Virgos, extremely dependable.*

Capricorn and Scorpio

Capricorn will plan and Scorpio will resist. Scorpio will scheme, and Capricorn will look on in amusement. I've certainly seen this work as a romantic combo, and though Scorpio sometimes thinks Capricorn is a little simplistic psychologically (not as challenging as a Gemini or Leo, to be sure), this can be a tranquil and successful pairing.

---

* Donna Lethal, email message to the author, October 2008.

Capricorn and Pisces

Capricorn can definitely supervise Pisces in a way that Pisces likes and sometimes needs a lifetime to come to terms with, believing they deserve. However, Pisces can be so sensitive, undisciplined, and artistic that Capricorn could find the abrupt changes of pace frustrating. These two signs are sixty degrees apart and can follow the earth-and-water pattern. They can accomplish a lot together as long as each of them understands the other has an extreme and regular need of solitude. Capricorn and Pisces can also share occasional bouts of gloominess. Because Pisces rules the 12th house (secrets and hidden places) and Capricorn is ruled by Saturn (all about limits), it can be a race to see who can cheer up more slowly.

Air Plus Water

Doesn't this make an easy image—bubbles, large and small! The bubble is an under-appreciated phenomenon—except by small children. And what do bubbles do? They amuse, they distract, and they represent activity going on beneath. Air and water sign people together can spark conversation and therefore sparkle together. Despite huge temperamental differences, at their best, these two elements can make for social merriment and enjoyable activities. This can be a romance that begins impetuously, and never achieves a "steady state."

Gemini and Scorpio

Gemini and Scorpio can have an amazing, kinetic interaction that before long, ends in misunderstandings. Here's a female Gemini on this combination: "I don't like working for Scorpios. They are usually secretive and their work agendas seem to concentrate around getting power for themselves." And here's a female Scorpio's response: "Geminis drive me *bananas*. They definitely have a split personality and just when you think you've got them figured out, they tip everything upside-down on you—like the one who stood me up on my birthday to go out with another woman." As arbiter in this slugfest, what I say to both of you is that if you want a relationship, you will both have periodic explosions due to Gemini changing their mind about what they thought they said, and Scorpio not being crystal-clear about their expectations. The Gemini will not figure things out alone; they need to be told. And told more than once, because they're not really paying attention.

Gemini and Pisces

This combo and the one after, Libra and Cancer, have built-in awkwardness, due to being square (ninety degrees) to one another. Then again, both can be perceived as willful. When it comes to sincerity, though, Pisces usually triumphs. Both signs can spend a lot of time analyzing the unpredictable aspects of the other but Gemini is usually better-suited to move on with life. Pisces, as a feeling-everything water sign, will often stay in this relationship past the point of sensibility. Usually, fish-folk figure out the two sides of the twins very early and then spend the rest of their time trying to accept it.

Libra and Cancer

See above. These signs are ninety degrees away, and their union is not—shall we say—the easiest or most obvious. Cancer can be *more* intense if they spend time with Libra, who in turn can seem more like a weather vane. Cancer wants to take things seriously and Libra likes to keep things light. Both are cardinal signs, and have a fair bit of direction. With prolonged exposure, both can overlook the parts of the other they initially liked. If the Cancer is a female and the Libra a male, there can be accommodations, in that Cancer infantalizes the Libra, and makes their choices for them, which takes away Libra anxiety. If the Cancer is a male and the Libra is a female, the Cancer can get frustrated if they don't think Libra is taking things seriously.

Libra and Pisces

Who's making the decisions here?! In the case of knockabout gagmen Bud Abbott and Lou Costello, the answer is their producer. Costello, the Pisces (March 6) was constantly befuddling Abbott, the Libra (October2), who only wanted order in an absurd world. "Who's on first" continues to delight middle school lads in every generation who can identify with the absurdist premise. Abbott, a classic straight man, vertical where Costello was spherical, is an identifiable Scales person, forever tied to someone who's like a fish swimming in opposite directions. I love the fact that Groucho Marx (October 2) shares Abbott's birthday, but, in combination with his cuspy crazy brothers Chico (March 22, early Aries) and Harpo (November 23, early Sagittarius), he could easily join in the mayhem.

Seriously, though, the air plus water combination will always make for an effervescent mix, and on an artistic or business level, this combination can be terrific. However, in my experience, when these two get together for romance, both are likely to defer to the other when it's time to make decisions. Unless Pisces is really close to Aries or Taurus, they'll figure Libra calls the shots. Libra close to Virgo is more comfortable being in charge, but honestly, both of these signs are basically craving someone with some stable earth to ground them!

Aquarius and Cancer

Aquarius may be a fixed sign and somewhat set in their ways, but compared to the crab—there is *no* contest here! This is another one of those partial opposites-attract combos I see among clients frequently. Aquarius has a blithe side and will not notice events that vex and beset Cancer. The crab can be a real watchdog for Aquarius, which can make the crab a little jumpy. Some Aquarians understand that the Cancer in the relationship is more than happy to pick up the pieces, attend to details, and keep track of the agenda, which leaves them freer to pursue the business of charming the masses.

I can give you no more successful pairing of these signs than our fortieth president, Ronald Reagan (February 6) and his second wife, Nancy (July 6). Ronald's career was in the doldrums when he met "Mommy" (as he came to call her), but with her drive and connections, he showed a renewed interest in performance and later, politics. After the 1985 assassination attempt on his life, Nancy quietly ran the Oval Office, a fact kept from the public until many years later, when various administration staff (and Nancy's astrologer, the brilliant Joan Quigley) shared their recollections. Nancy was protective and loyal to Ron, and also encouraged him to have deeper relationships with individuals than he might have wanted, most famously with the Gorbachevs. Whether or not you admire the work they did in the White House, the fact remains is that these two set the mark for air and water to have a lasting and passionate relationship.

Aquarius and Scorpio

Aquarius isn't always concerned with the details and Scorpio strategizes endlessly. If you think about these two elements in terms of proximity, there's a considerable natural distance. Air rises—into space. Water flows deep into the earth. For these two elements to forge a useful relationship, each has to understand that the other's traits will be utterly distinct from their own. Because both are fixed signs, each can be set in his or her ways, something the partner finds exasperating. If passion is meant to be sustained for a lengthy period of time, they must be fascinated with each other's mysteries and unpredictable nature.

Nevertheless, there can be mutual respect and enormous productivity in this pairing despite the ever-present tension. Susan B. Anthony (February 15) and Elizabeth Cady Stanton (November 12) were lifelong partners in the nineteenth century feminist movement. Both wrote copiously, but Susan was always a step ahead—she was unmarried, while Stanton managed a large household. Both were riveting speakers; together they accomplished more than they could have individually. Here's another interesting pair from last century: Henry Irving (February 6), the great actor/impresario was managed brilliantly by the publicity-conscious Bram Stoker (November 8). Stoker, who largely based *Dracula* on Irving's personality, had an appreciation of the darker side of theater. Scorpio, as we know, definitely enjoys any occupation that uses their analytical skills and Irving had the confidence and conviction (egomania?) of the visionary.

nine

ASTRO-ELEMENTAL GIFT GIVING

Never fret over buying a present again!

For some years in my "Moon Signs" column, I have presented gift-giving suggestions for various holidays (Christmas, Valentine's Day, Mother's Day, birthdays). Every year, there would be something new to add. Some signs (earth, mostly) are in a year-round gift-hunting mode, so when the biggest gift-giving season approaches, they not only are seldom caught short, but are thrilled to announce they're all done *weeks* before the first snowflake hits the ground.

Here are some suggestions on what those nearest and dearest might like . . .

Aries

This sign has enormous tolerance for joke gifts (receiving or giving), and can be great fun to shop for. Impulse gifts can satisfying the ram's child-like nature; also gifts that come in bright colors like red, orange, and yellow. Aries also is associated with wrought iron, so patio furniture, fireplace andirons, or small home furnishings such as coat hooks would also be winners.

Since Aries rules the head, you can't go wrong with a hat, especially one that advertises a passion or team. One of my much-treasured ancient astrology books helpfully provides herbs that are associated with each of the planets. Aries gets flaxseed (great for digestion), red pepper and peppermint (for their irresistible spicy personalities), and hops, among dozens more. Why not get a pillow filled with hops and aromatic herbs for the restless insomniac ram?

Taurus

Acquisitive and possessive, you can't go wrong getting a luxury item for people born under the sign of the bull. Chances are, your Taurus friend or family member collects something or has dozens of different collections, so providing another little china pig or stained-glass panel will prompt a smile. Taurus rules the second house, which includes personal and financial security issues. Why not a piggy bank made of nonstandard material? The body part ruled by Taurus is the throat, so a scarf made of luxurious material, a necklace, turtleneck sweaters or jerseys, neckties, or even a Nehru jacket would be welcome. Throat lozenges for the inevitable bout of laryngitis are sure to be used.

I've known Taurus folks with impulses towards austerity, but when it comes right down to it, they value quality and would rather have a small, well-made object rather than something large that was mass produced. The herbs and plants associated with Venus (Taurus' ruler) are apples, cherries, plums, poppies, violets, and burdock, daisy, holly, mint, cowslip, and cloves. Taurus has their birthday just as the violets and lilies of the valley are blooming, so a perfume, sachet, or actual plants would be welcome. At Christmas time, a child could put cloves in an orange for a Taurus relative.

Gemini

Surprise me! Oh wait, you didn't get me what I asked for! Shopping for Gemini can be an exercise straight out of Lewis Carroll's playbook. One minute, you're standing on the ground; the next moment, you're tumbling through the rabbit hole, en route to an exciting and occasionally aggravating place: Gemini-land! Twins people will test your listening skills, because they might idly say they always thought they'd love a lime-green sweater, and when you turn up with one in evergreen, they'll say thanks with a weak little smile (hot tip: if you get them a green sweater, get them something pink to go with it. Gems love the unexpected compromise).

This sign rules the third house of peer relationships and siblings. The body part Gemini controls is the lungs. That air sign quality (like Aquarius and to a lesser extent Libra) of being highly aware of trends means a CD or download by the coolest new singer could be just what tickles their fancy. If you really want to score big, give them something connected to information gathering or analyzing. Gems have a powerful aptitude for understanding computer programs that excite them. When I think back on the rise of the answering machine—from seventeen-second tape numbers that went *ka-chunk* as they started, to mini-tapes, to digital, to the rise of the smartphone, my recollection is that the first person on the block who had the Latest Thing was always a Gemini.

Miniature technology is a favorite, and so is, oddly enough, antique technology. I've known some Gemini record collectors who think the whole recording industry went to hell after transistors were phased in after tube amps. Continue with the communication theme, and a box of high-end designer stationery with an old-fashioned fountain pen (or a box of neon pencils—or both!) could amuse.

Herbs and plants within Mercury's realm are aromatic and practical: anise, dill, oats, savory, wild carrots, endive, wild celery. These are all in season when Gems have their birthday, so you could serve up a tasty salad and explain the lore later!

Cancer

Super, super easy to shop for. As long as the present shows you care, and that you know them (or want to know them), they're sold. This water sign rules the fourth house of home and hearth, and the predominant body part in its realm is the stomach. Basically, anything that enhances their home, makes it more cozy, or feeds them would be perfect. The kitchen is Cancer's natural place (and yes, I've known Cancers who don't cook, but usually they take pride in rustling up soup when they need to), so your shopping for them could include useful, basic, high-quality cookware. A set of durable metal measuring spoons, nesting measuring cups, or a handsome ceramic platter for them to display fruit would be welcome. So would a pastry board or wooden bread board. Cancerians can be excellent bakers (Cancer actually rules that profession), so a basic book on breads as well as some artisan flour (if your crabbie really likes to bake, instead of just talking about it) would be winning.

Continuing with the kneading theme, Cancers also have a sensual side and if you give them massage oil, prepare to use it—or let them use it on you. Luxury ingredients, or a gift along the lines of fruit of the month will also remind them you care. Whatever you do, don't expect big thanks if Cancer thinks you haven't put yourself out. Author Paul Burrell, aide-de-camp to the late Princess of Wales, describes her last birthday:*

> [Kensington Palace] resembled a florist's shop again: around fifty separate arrangements of fresh flowers, dried flowers, and plants took over every vase and pot. But the present that meant the most to the Princess was a phone call from a friend in America who'd woken at three a.m. specially to wish Diana a happy birthday at eight, British time. That is the devotion of a true friend.

---

* Paul Burrell, *A Royal Duty* (New York: Putnam 2003).

The plants and herbs that fall under the Moon's influence (Cancer's home planet) include some of the more arcane botanical specimens: Adder's tongue, the *Agaricus* family of mushrooms, Mercury moonwort, saxifrage, as well as many plants found in or near water: purple loosestrife, duckweed, watercress, water arrowhead, water lily, and iris. Honeysuckle is also included and ladies of a certain generation might be delighted at a gift of honeysuckle perfume or dusting powder.

Leo

Is it neon? Can I share it with fifty of my closest friends? Does it make me look *fabulous*? Buying for Leo can be an adventure for the insightful. Something sentimental or something sporty. Something that speaks to the child or the leader. Lion folks are ruled by the Sun and the heart is their domain. So is their hair, actually, so you may score points by finding some specialty hair care products such as shampoo and conditioner. Accoutrements could also be appreciated, like a good-for-a-lifetime boar-bristle brush, elegant barrettes or hair ties or ribbons. Of course, some Leos dispense with hair vanity and prefer to focus on other attributes. So think about clothing that emphasizes the heart area (and yes, this can include the bosom). I've known a few Leo brides who were thrilled to receive gorgeous lingerie at the bridal shower. Even the sportiest Leo has a side that wants to be grown-up and kingly (or queenly).

Specific gifts that speak to the fifth house themes of children and parties could be vintage games that still pack an entertainment wallop, particularly for large groups (Twister, Apples to Apples . . .). Also, presents that you'd think would work for a much younger person. A miniature remote control car for the office-bound executive, or an interesting antique incense burner (Leo is a fire sign, and can be fond of creating an atmosphere using interesting and flattering light sources). Since Leo also likes to be the authority, you might consider a subscription to a specialty magazine, or a shortwave radio so they can tune in to a variety of news stations.

Herbs and plants ruled by the Sun are just what you'd think would thrive under Sol's nurturing rays: calendula, chamomile, marigold, olive, orange, passion flower, sunflower. Calendula is a floral smell that has depth without being musky, and a skin cream in this flavor could be appreciated.

Virgo

You will not be able to out-gift these folks—for the most part, they just get you in a way you'll never get them. At best, gifts from a Virgo are just plain brilliant; at the least, they speak to an aspect of yourself you don't usually consider. Virgo will also fret and plan endlessly about whether their choice is smart enough. Meanwhile, the rest of us are left high and dry, trying to get something for the person we know who is practical, eclectic, and highly critical—pretty intimidating! Virgo rules the sixth house of health, work, and service matters and the most significant part of the body under its dominion is the lower intestine. Though none of this may sound very glamorous or "gift-able," put on a Virgo thinking cap and use your analytical skills. Finding out Virgo's favorite charity and donating in their name would earn approval. So would objects to help them do their work, or present a different persona in the workplace. What about a beautiful leather or durable briefcase to replace the backpack they're still using from college? Virgo sometimes professes disdain for objects that are too "designery," but they have a deep appreciation for quality.

As for that health category, perhaps a collection of vitamin sample packs, a DVD on the latest exercise technique, or an hour with a personal trainer. Virgo can also veer into hypochondriac territory, so travel-size hand sanitizer or wipes could be an amusing (and appreciated) stocking stuffer for the Virgo who interacts with the public. Virgo, like Gemini, is ruled by Mercury and the herbs and plants that strike me as essentially Virgo-like would be: balm (melissa—useful for skin care), caraway (great for digestion), parsley (ditto), wintergreen (breath freshener), and to soothe fretting tendencies, lavender. An herbal garden with these plants could bring out their nurturing side.

Libra

Oh, don't ask me to make a list—I couldn't tell you what item I really love best! Libra can be the easiest person to shop for because they're so indecisive, any item you present to them (which, of course, represents a decision) could rack up big points. Libra dominates the seventh house, partnerships, but also personal identity within an intimate relationship. It's an air sign ruled by Venus, opposite Aries. Its body part includes the not-so-glamorous bladder and urinary area. You can't generalize about this sign more than the others except in this one key way: Libra, even if they are longtime anchorites, are, in their own heads, needing to be attached to another. Over the years, I've known Libras who were addicted to relationship books, or any information to help them understand the vagaries of intimacy.

Because Libra is ruled by Venus, who concerns herself with love and friendship issues, Libra can be extremely well groomed and totally put together. Or, partially so. The ironed shirt and wrinkly skirt—the flawless makeup and dark-at-the-roots hairdo. Gifts for Libra can speak to their appetites or their aesthetic sense. If you give a Libra a framed picture, chances are they'll hang it up. If you give them an unframed picture, they'll agonize about what frame is perfect. Thus, sets or pre-assembled ensembles make them happy. The bath set with the matching fragrance, soap, and cream—there are three decisions you've saved them!

With a Venus rulership, herbs and plants under that dominion tend to be pretty: columbine, daisy, holly, cowslip, verbena, and violets. A Libra child might enjoy learning needlework with a pattern of those blooms.

Scorpio

Okay, now we're in interesting, exciting, and provocative territory. Scorpio gets so much heat for ruling the eighth house—"sex, death and other people's money"—that you think they would turn up their noses at anything less exotic than bondage gear and a bag of Krugerrands. Yet, there's a nurturing side to many Scorpios that they conceal with varying degrees of success. I've known some very prickly and difficult Scorpios who turned out to be secret cactus growers. Or those who had no patience with human beings, yet who managed to keep a flock of African violets, that dainty and delicate little plant, flourishing for years. ("Water from the bottom" is what they always say, but I know they're doing some magic mojo.) Plants that thrive on neglect can be a good gift for a Scorpio (in keeping with the resurrection theme). Pickling is a Scorpio pursuit, also wallets or containers for money. Purses made of quirky material, like duct tape or wood, could catch their fancy.

Keeping with the themes of growth and nurturing, a Scorpio who likes to putter in the kitchen could be thrilled with a home-brew kit, or a make-your-own-sushi kit. Cooking, you say? Actually, sushi preparation touches on some primo Scorpionic themes—the manipulation of sharp knives, for example, as Scorpio rules surgery.

You could always skip the practicalities and go straight to lush, decadent luxury. Dark chocolate versus milk; perfume versus cologne; wool or silk versus cotton; leather versus plastic . . . you get the idea. As for that sharp Scorpio tongue, a book of snappy comebacks could be a guilty pleasure. If you're visiting the desert, you can give them a moment's pause by bringing back one of those paperweights sold in tourist trap gift shops with the resin-encased scorpion.

Pluto is Scorpio's ruler, although for centuries Scorpio shared Mars with Aries. Scorpio's body parts are the genitals and organs of reproduction, which definitely gets into the realm of *personal* gifts. Depending on your comfort level, you might try a lacy Victorian nightgown or maybe a pair of fuzzy handcuffs. Plants and herbs considered to be Scorpionic would be cat mint, mustard, myrtle, pine, and sarsaparilla.

Sagittarius

"Fun, fun, fun 'til Daddy took the T-bird away." And then Sagittarius called up one of their friends and went joy-riding in *their* hot rod! Getting a great gift for a Sagittarius can be one of your most entertaining adventures. Sadge's domain is the ninth house, which includes higher education, long trips, and exotic cultures ("exotic" meaning not your own). Jupiter is the ruler, and since Jove is one of the most generous spirits in the universe, you can make Sagittarians feel appreciated by finding out their pet charity and sending a contribution (hint: at-risk overseas children, or disability groups).

The body part Sagittarius governs is the hips and thighs to around the knee area. Thus belts or items of clothing that emphasize this part of the body are a good fit. Yoga pants, or specialty trousers for a particular occupation or activity would work. Legwarmers are never out of style for folks who live north of Washington DC. And since Sagittarius has an adventurous side, an introductory horseback or skiing lesson could inspire them—ditto great walking shoes. With their taste for adventure, try travel books, atlases, or travel journals. Some excellent authors include Evelyn Waugh, Dervla Murphy, Lawrence Millman, and even Osbert Sitwell. If your Sadge isn't a big reader, consider getting some exotic snacks from a country they're never likely to visit. Candy or sweets from Asia, or condiments from the Indian subcontinent can make them feel exotic. Don't forget: Sagittarius is the centaur. Do they have room for an archery set?

Jupiter is Sagittarius' ruler, and the plants and herbs this sign has an affinity for include: apricot, asparagus, bilberry, cinquefoil (a really nice herbaceous border), myrrh, oak, peppermint, sage, salvia, and every child's favorite traveling plant: the dandelion.

Capricorn

Practical, capable, eccentric Capricorn. They don't mind cheap, but they do mind thoughtless. They may not remember to get you a gift, but if they do, it would be of the highest quality, at a very good price. Their symbol is the goat and Capricorn rules the tenth house, which includes public face/career/success and limits. Capricorn likes durable goods and since it's a sign that also rules structure, a little Capricorn child could use blocks, Legos, or any construction material. Older Caps might like glass bricks or room dividers, and the really handy Caps would be ecstatic to receive a gift certificate to their favorite home construction supply store; even a pallet full of cinderblocks would be used.

I know a practical Cap furniture restorer who has no use for chocolate or champagne, but gets misty at the site of a broken-down 1950s wooden Danish modern coffee table in need of restoration. Capricorns are the natural fixers of the zodiac, and the best lesson you can teach them early is money management. A piggy bank might be fine, but a savings bond or mutual fund with a maturation date would have a different impact. Capricorn rules the knees down to the ankles, so boots or hiking socks or practical footwear could be their thing. Last but not least, chèvre would be a delicious gift.

Saturn is Capricorn's ruler, and Saturnian plants and herbs are aconite, aspen, barley, belladonna, comfrey, ivy, onion, and solomon's seal.

Aquarius

This is another fun person to buy presents for, but one where I hesitate to generalize. Aquarians are so individual and eccentric that the sentimental tchotchke that rings the bell of one will leave another indifferent. Ruling the eleventh house (friends, hopes and wishes), Aquarians can be highly trend-conscious, so the latest best-selling self-help book could be an ideal amusement for the Christmas season. Don't forget, they have their birthday around Valentine's Day, so you can't go wrong getting them a Valentine-themed birthday present, particularly if they are—like so many adorable, irresistible Aquarians—happily solitary.

The body part governed by this sign is the calf and ankle area, so sets of novelty ankle socks, in a rainbow of colors could be a practical, whimsical gift. The other areas controlled by Aquarius are electricity and mass movements. Again, a quirky lighting source or books on trends or alternative energy will provide ample food for thought. I've also known Aquarians who are touched and soothed by a gift of a tabletop fountain (hey, despite being an air sign they *are* the water carrier). Communication is key to all the air signs, so a novelty phone, like one of those in the shape of a football or high-heeled shoe, might be appreciated. Gauge your Aquarian carefully—some of them are utterly besotted with fantasy or sci-fi themes.

Uranus is their planet and that planet is *so* far away that it doesn't really have any plants and herbs directly associated with it. However, bearing in mind the themes of trend-setting, nervous issues, and the body parts of calf and ankle, herbs that speak to these issues will be thoughtful.

Pisces

Our last sign doesn't expect much. Really, you shouldn't have bothered. This is for me? Really? That's so sweet. I wish I'd gotten you something. Pisces can give a variety of responses as far as gift-giving goes, but you can't go wrong with a few themes. Since the twelfth house covers unconscious impulses, the subconscious, and hidden places, camera equipment or books about photography are winners. So are books about life at the bottom of the ocean, picture books about prisons or sanitariums (I'm not kidding), or Woodstock, which, despite its Age of Aquarius theme was definitely a Pisces event, particularly when the mud pits started.

Pisces has an affinity for all kinds of music, so music from child-hood (i.e. nostalgic tunes) will score big, as well mood music. During the sixties, virtually every rock band had a psychedelic album, and I've never met a Pisces who didn't adore *Sgt. Pepper, Dark Side of the Moon,* and anything by Nirvana (led by fellow fish, the late Kurt Cobain). You can have a lot of fun buying presents for Pisces because they rule the feet: think shoes, sandals, and boots. Wait—how about an aquarium? No, more thoughtful is the artificial human equivalent, the lava lamp, containing nothing living.

Neptune is Pisces' ruler and this planet of dreaminess, distraction, and escape has some *very interesting* herbs under its guidance. You will probably want to forgo products from the coca and poppy plants, but some high quality coffee beans are a perfectly Piscean gift.

CONCLUSION

Fire, earth, air, water. That's where we start, and that's where we end. If you've come this far, you probably have a handle on the basics of the elements, and if I've done my job, you have become more alert to the distinctions between each of the three signs in each element.

When in doubt with astrology, keep it simple. Go back to the basics. Have the mental image of each sign and element in view when you try to analyze someone's motives, or plan to ask for a favor, or want to write a love letter. I deliberately excluded ramifications of Ascendants, Moons, and other planets in this book because I want you, the reader (to whom this book is dedicated), to get comfortable with the basic concepts. If you want to explore astrology in greater depth, there are many excellent authors to read and I mention several in my Acknowledgements page.

If I've *really* done my job, you should have a better understanding of your own potential and proclivities. People are more than capable of surprising you, but generally are most comfortable in their comfort zone. Which is to say that your multitasking, high-function, mile-a-minute personalities are likely to have some air going on, and your impatient, initiating types who want to lead probably have a touch of fire. Meanwhile, your slower, plodding, patient types have some earth in their background, and those who are perceptive about others' feelings rather than actions are likely to be somewhat aquatic, if not totally watery.

IMPORTANT
ASTROLOGICAL TERMS

Some of these terms aren't in this book, but if you continue to study astrology, you will definitely want to know some basic definitions.

ANGLES (in order of increasing magnitude)—The angles in your chart refer directly to the geometric angles between the planets. A basic understanding of geometry is helpful in astrology—and I mean *really* basic. A circle is 360 degrees. There are twelve signs and twelve houses. Each of these takes up around thirty degrees in a chart.

Conjunction: Planets in the same sign. Three or more and you have a stellium. You can be a fire sign, and with a sprinkling of planets in lots of water signs, you become the most sensitive and impulsive one of your circle.

Semi-sextile: The sign within thirty degrees, ergo, the sign next door. There's a chapter on astrological neighbors that goes into detail. Suffice to say, many signs are highly tolerant of their closest sign.

Octile, also known as *semi-square:* Signs that are forty-five degrees apart. We're halfway to a square, and sometimes this can be a harmonious moment in time. Figure this is the moment between a semi-sextile and a sextile.

Sextile: Signs within sixty degrees. And yes, sometimes comes with "sex." Signs sixty degrees apart are considered highly compatible and harmonious. This means that your earth sign syncs up with a water sign, or your fire sign syncs up with an air sign. But wait—think about it: too much earth and water can make for sludginess in behavior, and too much fire and air makes for inconsistency and unreliability.

Quintile: Signs seventy-two degrees apart. Relates to "quincunx," which is twice as far. My jury is still out on the meaningfulness of this, but if you use it for horary astrology—projecting forward on projects—it can be useful as the date is nearly two and a half months forward, or ten weeks, the time of many semesters in school. But like I said, it's not a configuration I've been using a lot.

Square: Signs that are ninety degrees apart. Considered challenging, but also useful if those signs are ruled by Mars or Jupiter or Saturn. People who have to struggle a little bit harder usually have a lot of squares in their chart.

Trine: Signs that are 120 degrees apart, which means they're in the same element. A proliferation of trines usually confers natural talent or ease. People with more trines than squares sometimes have an easier time in the world and don't have to fight for everything. Does this make you a better person? It depends, but it can certainly make you more relaxed.

Sesqui-quadrate: Now we're getting into the higher math. This sign is 135 degrees away from another. If you're looking at one date and the next date is four months away, that's this angle.

Biquintile: Signs that are 144 degrees away from one another, or nearly five months apart.

Quincunx: Signs that are 150 degrees away from one another and a recurrent theme, at least in the astrology I do and the clients to whom I speak. Defying rational explanation, the signs that have a quincunx relationship usually have a blind spot where the other is concerned. I always project this forward, so Capricorn is quincunx with Leo mostly, although 150 degrees from Capricorn in the *other* direction is Gemini. Let's go through these, and please look at the blurb on "Leo/Capricorn" as an example. Sign quincunx to Aries is Virgo (also Scorpio). Sign quincunx to Taurus is Libra (also Sagittarius). Sign quincunx to Gemini is Scorpio (also Capricorn). Sign quincunx to Cancer is Sagittarius (also Aquarius). Sign quincunx to Leo is Capricorn (also Pisces). Sign quincunx to Virgo is Aquarius (also Aries). Sign quincunx to Libra is Pisces (also Taurus). Sign quincunx to Scorpio is Aries (also Gemini). Sign quincunx to Sagittarius is Taurus (also Cancer). Sign quincunx to Capricorn is Gemini (also Leo). Sign quincunx to Aquarius is Cancer (also Virgo). Sign quincunx to Pisces is Leo (also Libra).

Opposition: Signs that are 180 degrees away from one another. The natural oppositions in the zodiac are Aries/Libra, Taurus/Scorpio, Gemini/Sagittarius, Leo/Aquarius, and Virgo/Pisces. I wrote a whole chapter on these interactions; have another look. It is totally *not* a deal-breaker if you are one sign and someone you like, love, work with, or are obsessed with is the opposite sign. Think of how magnetic polarity works, and be reassured.

Stellium: Three or more planets in a sign. This totally tips the balance in a chart and can potentially undermine the Sun sign unless the stellium is in the Sun sign. For example, former president Bill Clinton has a stellium of planets in his first house, which is Libra. There's Mars, Neptune, Venus, and Jupiter all within seventeen degrees of one another (there's also Chiron, for those who use that planet). With so much activity in Libra, Bill's Leo Sun has always been compromised and equivocation helps undermine that Leo leadership.

ASCENDANT—Your rising sign or the sign on the cusp of the first house. This is how the world perceives you and what they pick up on. You can be a deeply feeling water sign, but if you have an earth sign Ascendant, others think you're more decided than you are. Or if you are an earth sign with an air sign Ascendant, your friends might think you're more flexible than you are.

ELEMENTS—This info is *all* over this book, but okay . . . you need a quick summary.

Fire: passion, impulse, excitement, initiative

Earth: consistency, reliability, groundedness, sensuality

Air: inventiveness, improvisation, communication, spaciness

Water: flexibility, sensitivity, recessiveness, perception

HOUSES—I'll give you definitions as I would give to a client. If you are going to get more serious about studying astrology and get your natal chart and start analyzing, take a step back and think of *yourself* as your first client. Understanding what the planets mean *and* what the houses mean will truly give you the keys to the kingdom. When you look at your chart for the first time and find your eyes crossing and that "I didn't study for this exam" feeling, take a step back. The most important thing to learn first is that a horoscope is to be read as if it were a backwards-running clock that begins at nine o'clock. So the first house starts at nine and goes to eight o'clock. The second house goes from eight to seven o'clock or so (houses are not as geometrically exact as we would have them!). The third house goes from seven to six o'clock, and the fourth house starts at six o'clock, which is also the *Immum Coeli*, or bottom of the chart.

1st house: Your Ascendant, which represents what you project to the world, what the world sees. Basic identity. Relates to Aries.

2nd house: Material security, banking, what you have. Refers to your relationship or need for financial/emotional security. Relates to Taurus.

3rd house: Peers, siblings, communication, and short trips. Planets here tell me how you get along with other folks in a general way, and how effective you are at communication. Relates to Gemini.

4th house: The house, home base, also, strangely, your father and old age. Relates to Cancer.

5th house: Children or childish pursuits, pleasure, speculation or willingness to take chances, risk-taking. Relates to Leo.

6th house: Work, service, charities, health, and your relationship to these important concepts. Relates to Virgo.

7th house: Also known as the Descendant (it's opposite your ascendant). Marriage and partnerships, also enemies you're aware of, sometimes law suits, also public relations. Relates to Libra.

8th house: Sex, death, and other people's money (I love writing that). Okay, how about: physical intimacy, your relationship with those in the great beyond, wills, probate, legacies and inheritances. Relates to Scorpio.

9th house: Higher education, spiritual and religious pursuits, long journeys (by sea, traditionally). Relates to Sagittarius.

10th house: Profession and/or social standing in the world. This is the natural progression from the 9th house—you study, and then you practice. Also relates to the mother (versus the father, which you'd think would be here, with the mother in the Cancerian or nurturing post, but astrology is never as cut and dried as you'd hope). This is also the Midheaven, or the top of the chart. Relates to Capricorn.

11th house: Friends, hopes, wishes, dreams, aspirations. How you get along with large groups of people or groupthink. Relates to Aquarius.

12th house: Secrets, hidden places, the things we want to keep hidden, secret enemies, the unconscious, the spiritual unknown, the mysteries and unknowable things. Relates to Pisces.

PLANETS

Sun: 365-day orbit. Who you are. It's that simple. Leo's planet.

Moon: 29.5-day orbit. Your emotional responsiveness, how your feelings work, what you respond to on a visceral versus intellectual level. Also can define or explain maternal instincts or your relationship with your mom or mom stand-ins. Cancer's planet.

Mercury: 88-day orbit. How you communicate. This is always in your Sun sign or the sign before or after. If you are born with natal Mercury retrograde, you might have an affinity for the following: people who do not speak your language as a first language; those who do not communicate as others do (e.g., the deaf, autistic, or mentally challenged, also stroke victims). You'll be at your best when Mercury is retrograding, and you should expect to explain things more than once. Natal Mercury retrograde can also indicate a talent for nonverbal communicatinon (e.g., musical or artistic ability). See "Retrograde" further along in this section for more. Gemini and Virgo's planet.

Venus: 225-day orbit. How you respond to friends, loved ones, aesthetic experiences, things that make you feel good. What your taste is like. Can be in your Sun sign or the sign before or after, and, less often, two signs away from your Sun sign. In the charts of straight men, this is one of the indicators along with the Moon, as to the kind of female they want to spend time with. Ditto for gay women. Taurus and Libra's planet.

Mars: 687-day orbit. How you take action—are you brave, impulsive, retiring, irritable, excitement-craving? Mars gets back to its natal place every two years, prompting a massive round of decisiveness, and conjuncts your Sun every two years or so (prompting a need to take action, and occasionally an accident-prone period). In straight women, the sign and element this planet is in can incline one towards partners of similar sign or element. In gay men, this is who will rock your socks off. Aries' planet (used to be Scorpio's also).

Jupiter: 12-year orbit. How you are generous, how you are willing to give back to others and the world. What your capacity is for thinking beyond yourself. I think of Jupiter and Saturn as being the good and bad uncles at a christening. Jupiter will urge you to enjoy your life and *carpe diem*. Saturn will urge you to save your money and not to expect those good times to last. Sagittarius' planet.

Saturn: 29.5-year orbit. How you set limits or how limits are set in your life. What your endurance is like. How prone you are to depression or anxiety. How willing you are to work hard. Can also indicate how you perceive paternal figures in your life. This is the planet that the ancient astrologers looked at with great trepidation. But you have *got* to love Saturn and, at some point in your life, befriend someone with a decent telescope so you can see the little gasbag with its rings and moons. For the ancients, however, there was no more baleful planet, and I still have to stop myself from underestimating its effects, particularly on clients who are under age thirty. I find the Saturnian intervals useful when talking to folks. Expect life changes at 27–29 years. If you want to look at the intervals of Saturnian shifts and upheaval, start reducing these figures. That 29-year Saturn return divided in half brings major change every 13 to 14 years. But you can also expect your life to shift every 6.5 to 7 years. Also, 3.5 years can be potent—I've known many people in business who are climbing the walls, wanting to be "farther along" after three-and-a-half years. Divide that in half and you get 21 months (a year and nine months), a useful time to complete coursework or a payment plan! Keep dividing, and you can make shifts at 10.5 months and my personal favorte, 3.5 months, which roughly corresponds to the semester system in college. We crave change and also fear it; finding a healthy middle path using these Saturnian periods can help with transition.

The Outer Planets

These are planets that allow you to fine-tune your understanding of your chart. Their orbits are so long they end up being generational markers. However, their relationship to other planets is crucial.

Uranus: 84-year orbit. Folks who have Uranus in a square or awkward position to Sun or Venus often have eccentric tastes in friends, for example. I've found that elderly people can be in a particularly vulnerable period health-wise between age 82 and 84. This is a period where life gets very simple and postponed health issues can catch up with you. Aquarius' planet.

Neptune: 165-year orbit. Your proclivity to walk (and talk) on the wild side. Artistic inclinations, the need to escape. Neptune in the first house can be a marker for alcoholic or excessive behaviors. Pisces' planet.

Pluto: 248-year orbit (but a variable and unpredictable path). It is above the plane of the ecliptic of the other planets. And though it was tremendously sad to see the little rock get downgraded not so long ago, it's still a planet by my lights. Pluto is very helpful when you're looking at a chart. It's a generational marker and spends decades in a sign. However, the angle it makes to other planets and its house placement give me an indication where a client has an "I don't care, burn down the house" impulse. Scorpio's planet.

RETROGRADE—If people know just a tiny bit about astrology, the first concept they respond to is the idea of retrograde. The late Darrell Martinie, formerly of Boston's WBCN, pioneered the use of this phrase in his broadcasts on the station in the 1970s and 1980s, making an entire region alert to the concept of Mercury retrograde. Retrograde is actually a perceptual concept versus an astronomical actuality. Because of where we are on planet Earth, and where the planets are in our solar system, periodically we get into relationships with one another that makes it *look* like the planets are not moving (stationary) or moving backwards (retrograde). Of course we *know* no planet ever changes direction, but the ancients had to explain this apparent astronomical impossibility and interpret it, ergo the idea that planetary influence diminishes, reverses, or implodes during retrograde periods.

Mercury is our most frequent and regular retrograder. It "reverses" direction for three weeks twice a year or so. During this time, its influence becomes troublesome, particularly in the fields of communication. You'll want to avoid signing contracts, upgrading communication or electronic equipment, launching a marketing plan, or finalizing an agreement. This period also has some usefulness: think of Mercury retrograde periods as unanticipated vacations from onerous decision making or problem solving. This can be a useful period for artistic or creative endeavors. It's also a time when the unexpected is a natural occurrence and coincidences have an amusing flair.

My personal Mercury retrograde story goes like so: I married my husband during Mercury retrograde. We didn't plan it—we chose an interval of time when family members would be available, and it was smack in the middle of Mercury retrograde. Our travel plans were fine, our guests arrived on time, the cake lady came early and made everything look pretty, and then my mother threw out the marriage license and needed to go Dumpster diving in the middle of the night. Her explanation: "I was cleaning up." Granted, the license was in a FedEx envelope, so that might have looked like junk, but it was a quirky and absurd conclusion. Had my mom not fessed up, I wonder whether we would still be legally married without the document!